Charles Stedman Newhall

Harry's Trip to the Orient

Charles Stedman Newhall
Harry's Trip to the Orient
ISBN/EAN: 9783337149109

Printed in Europe, USA, Canada, Australia, Japan

Cover: Foto ©Andreas Hilbeck / pixelio.de

More available books at **www.hansebooks.com**

Harry's
Trip to the Orient.

BY

REV. CHARLES STEDMAN NEWHALL.

AMERICAN TRACT SOCIETY,
150 NASSAU STREET, NEW YORK.

COPYRIGHT, 1885,
BY AMERICAN TRACT SOCIETY.

CONTENTS.

CHAPTER I.
Before Sailing. Planning. Letters. Cousin Will . . . 7

CHAPTER II.
Setting Sail. Telegram. The "Norman Monarch." "Under Way." The Captain. Broken Compass. Little Gull Reef 12

CHAPTER III.
On the Ocean. Storm and Calm. The "Snow Fall." The Azores 16

CHAPTER IV.
Across the Atlantic. St. Vincent's Light. Straits of Gibraltar. "The Rock." Donkey Ride 23

CHAPTER V.
Through the Mediterranean. Dardanelles and Sea of Marmora 30

CHAPTER VI.
Constantinople. The Dogs. Crowded Streets. The Bridge of the Golden Horn. The "Bible House." Dr. Wood . 37

CHAPTER VII.
Constantinople—*Continued.* St. Sophia 50

CHAPTER VIII.
Constantinople—*Continued.* Howling Dervishes. Whirling Dervishes 57

CHAPTER IX.
Coast of Asia Minor. Smyrna. The Castle. "Robbers." Polycarp 63

CHAPTER X.

Coast of Asia Minor — *Continued.* Scenery. Breakfast. Rhodes. Landing at Beirût 68

CHAPTER XI.

Beirût to Damascus. Lebanon. Scenery. Roads. Danger. Escape. Sthorer. Anti-Lebanon. Valley of Abana. Damascus 74

CHAPTER XII.

Damascus. Before Breakfast. Mount Kasiun. View. The Streets. "St. Joseph's Gate." Place of Paul's Conversion. "Triumphal Arch" 87

CHAPTER XIII.

Damascus—*Continued.* A Turkish Bath 96

CHAPTER XIV.

Damascus to Baalbec. "The Waterfall." A Quarrel. Andrea. Approach to Baalbec. "Good Morning" 100

CHAPTER XV.

Baalbec and Return to Beirût. The Ruins by Starlight. The Ruins by Daylight. Rough Riding. Meeting Friends. Horses and Men for Jerusalem 108

CHAPTER XVI.

Beirût to the Damur. The "Caravan." A "Prophet." Fishermen. Nooning by the Damur 115

CHAPTER XVII.

The Damur to Sidon. Jonah. Traditions. "Jonah's Tomb." Approach to Sidon. Imagined Talk with the "Spirit of Sidon." Searching for Lodgings. The Hospice. The Missionaries 124

CHAPTER XVIII.

Sidon to Tyre. Tombs. Nooning by the Litany. Approach to Tyre. Alexander's Causeway. Reception. Supper. Evening on the Cliffs 138

CHAPTER XIX.

Tyre to Acre. Early Start. "White Promontory." "Ladder of Tyre," "Râs en Nakûrah." View of the Plain of Acre. Approach to Acre. Rebellion. Acre . . . 152

CHAPTER XX.

A Night Ride to Haifa. Running Horses. The Belus. Murex Shells. Fording the Kishon 162

CHAPTER XXI.

Haifa to Carmel and Nazareth. Ascent of Carmel. Galilean Scenery. View of Nazareth. "Nazareth." Arrival. Fra Johannes. Night at the Franciscan Hospice . . . 173

CHAPTER XXII.

Nazareth to Tiberias. Good-by to Fra Johannes. Cana. A Typical Face. The "Horns of Hattin." First View of Gennesaret. "Galilee." The Battle of Hattin. Tiberias. Evening by the Lake. "Boat Song" . . . 187

CHAPTER XXIII.

The Shore of Gennesaret. Collision with a Camel. A Friendly Native. The "Witches' Tree." Magdala. The Plain of Gennesaret. A Camel Ride. Robbers of Arbela. Search for the "Round Fountain." Fount of the Fig-tree. Tabighah. Tell Hûm. "Shells." A Storm . . . 200

CHAPTER XXIV.

Mount Tabor 217

CHAPTER XXV.

Mount Tabor to Jezreel. Descent of Tabor. Endor. The Witches' Cave. Nain. Shunem. Jezreel 221

CHAPTER XXVI.

Jenin. A Night with the Natives 230

CHAPTER XXVII.

Jenin to Samaria and Nablûs 238

CHAPTER XXVIII.

Nablûs to Jerusalem. "Jacob's Well." Robbers' Cave. Mount Scopus. View of Jerusalem. "Tombs of the Kings." Arrival 247

CHAPTER XXIX.

Around Jerusalem. Bethlehem. Mount of Olives. Bethany. Gethsemane. "Under a Star" 254

CHAPTER XXX.

Sacred Sites. The Temple Area. Jews' Wailing-Place. Robinson's Arch. Church of the Holy Sepulchre . . 267

CHAPTER XXXI.

From Jerusalem to Jaffa. The "Quarries" under Jerusalem. Night Ride to Jaffa. Jaffa. The "Juno." Embarking . 278

CHAPTER XXXII.

Egypt 287

CHAPTER XXXIII.

Cairo 294

CHAPTER XXXIV.

A Sabbath Day in Cairo 302

CHAPTER XXXV.

Memphis: Tombs of the Sacred Bulls 308

CHAPTER XXXVI.

The Pyramids 322

CHAPTER XXXVII.

Alexandria. Home 336

HARRY'S TRIP TO THE ORIENT.

CHAPTER I.

BEFORE SAILING.

THERE had been a long silence in the bright study, while the father read and the mother and Mary were busy with their work, and Harry was thinking. The younger children were away in dream-land. Now the silence is broken.

"Father, may I go with Cousin Will to Palestine?"

"To Palestine! Why, Harry, what gave you that idea?" And the father deliberately takes off his glasses and looks at Harry, and then, after a long pause,

"Well, what do you say, mother?"

Harry's face brightens, but the mother only looks rather anxious. She does not speak.

"Write to Will to-morrow and find out what he thinks of it," the father says.

And Harry writes to Cousin Will that night. This is the letter:

"DEAR COUSIN WILL: May I go with you to Palestine? Father does not say I can, but he says, 'Write him about it,' and I think that almost means that he is willing for me to go if you are.

"Yours truly,
"HARRY HOWARD."

And by return mail came the answer:

"DEAR HARRY: Meet me, if you can, with the horses at the 5:30 train to-morrow.

"Yours,
"WILL HOWARD."

Harry pondered the answer, standing by his horse with bridle and letter in hand at the post-office. "It may mean," he thought, "that Cousin Will does not want to disappoint me by writing 'No,' so is coming to tell me 'No;' but I think it means the opposite; and if it does, then with him ready to let me go, and father rather inclined to let me go, and with mother only at first a little anxious, as I suppose all such good mothers are, and with Mary willing to trust me anywhere with Cousin Will, hurrah and hurrah and hurrah! I believe I am going to Palestine;" and so he mounts and gallops home.

Will has come. Harry has met him and welcomed him at the station, and all the household have welcomed him again most heartily as they drove up, a little later, to the home-door.

Now the family are sitting before the open fire talking of the proposed journey. Mr. Howard says,

"I only know, Will, that you are about to visit Palestine. Whether you could take Harry with you; whether the details of your plan are such that it would be best for him to go if you could take him, I do not know."

Will replies, "If Harry wants to go, and if you are willing to trust him when you have heard my plans, I shall be very glad to have him with me. But, aunt, how soon could he be ready? I may have to start within three days, though possibly not for a month or more."

"He can be ready in three days."

"Well, this is my plan: I am not going by the usual route, but instead shall sail directly for Constantinople, stopping only once on the way, for coal at Gibraltar. Our steamship is lying now at New Haven, loaded with ammunition and guns for the Turkish Government. The voyage will take about a month, and if March is March-like, it will be a stormy time. But the ship is strong and is thoroughly well officered, and it is comfortable, though not intended for a passenger ship. Harry, if he goes, and I will be the only passengers. Does any of that frighten you, Harry? A month, and possibly a month of storms!"

"No, indeed."

"The ship is the 'Norman Monarch.' I shall leave her at Constantinople, and after a few days sail again by the French line along the coast of Asia Minor to Beirût. There I shall be close by Bible lands, and will aim to see as much of them as possible. I shall go to Damascus and Baalbec, and then either back to Beirût and by steamer to Jaffa and up to Jerusalem, or else overland to Jerusalem. In returning I shall sail from Jaffa for Port Saïd, and after a week or two in Egypt shall come rapidly home by the usual route—to Naples and across the continent, and by steamship from Glasgow or Liverpool to New York. I expect to be away about six months. That is my itinerary."

"It sounds like a 'Table of Contents,'" suggested Mary.

"Ah, Will, it seems a long, long journey that you are undertaking," said mother.

Father said, "If you are prospered, it will surely be a most interesting one. Harry, are you certain you want to venture on a journey such as that, so far away and for so long a time?"

"Yes, sir, certain, if you and mother are willing."

And the mother made no objection. She said, "I will not keep you, my boy, though many, many times I shall be anxious for you; very anxious it would be, except that I know you will be well cared for. Will will do his part, and the rest, you know, is in God's hands."

And so it was decided.

Will would have to leave them in the morning. After the three days for loading the ship Harry must be watching for a telegram, he said, and ready to start any time at an hour's notice.

At family worship that evening there was new interest for them all in the Psalm which the father read, which declares that as the mountains are round about Jerusalem, so the Lord is round about his people, henceforth even for ever; and in the Scripture from the New Testament, which tells of how much greater value man is in the sight of the Heavenly Father than are the birds of the air, which never want for food, and the flowers of the field, which are arrayed as Solomon never was in all his glory. Harry thought of the time when he would stand before those mountains that are round about Jerusalem, and the mother was helped anew by the needed lesson of God's loving care.

CHAPTER II.

SETTING SAIL.

THE 11th of March was an eventful date in Harry's life. When he awoke that morning he heard the brown sparrows twittering in the yard, under the trees, and about the barn-doors, and could see them flying back and forth before his window. The next morning he would see no birds excepting white sea-gulls with yellow bills following in the wake of the ship. Here were the gray hills with the sun streaming over them; then the only hills would be the waves. Now there were a few clouds, like ships, drifting across the sky; then he would be in the ship drifting on the wide, wild ocean.

At noon of that day the door-bell rang. There stood the telegraph-boy with the expected telegram from Will. It read: "Ship is ready. Meet me in city by next train."

There was only time to finish the packing, to speak the good-bys, and hasten away to the cars.

At midnight Will and Harry and Mr. Howard were in New Haven; and early the next morning

SETTING SAIL.

Mr. Howard stood alone on the pier looking down the harbor, where a level line of black smoke streamed like a pennant from the smokestack of the "Norman Monarch" as she steamed out to sea with the travellers on board, beginning the long voyage which was to lead before its ending through many different waters and into far different lands.

At the same time the travellers stood on the quarter-deck looking back towards the pier, until the city, and finally its hills, were out of sight. Then Harry turned with interest to examine more closely what was to be for so long a time their floating home. He made friends with the captain at once.

"Can I come on the bridge with you, captain?"

"Yes, yes, my hearty; climb up. The ship's free to you. I know Mr. William, and I'll risk you."

Harry climbed one ladder to the first landing. Then he was opposite the doors of the wheelhouse. Then he climbed again up to the "bridge," where he could overlook the whole vessel from stem to stern.

"How steadily the ship moves, captain, and how still the water is! It does not seem as though there could ever be waves big enough to make the ship roll and plunge as they say ships sometimes do."

"Ay, ay, my hearty; but the water's asleep now. Look here. Do you see this compass, how heavily cased it is, and how it's held to its place by these three stout legs riveted to the deck?"

"Yes; but the glass is broken, and the frame and legs are all twisted out of place."

"What do you think did that? A wave did it! The compass stands twenty-five feet above the water; but in that storm we shipped a sea that smashed the compass and pitched the first officer into the lee netting and started the after cabin. That was on the last voyage over."

"The sea was awake that time, captain."

"Ay, ay, my hearty; there you're right; wide awake; livelier than you'd care to see it, was n't it?"

Harry thought not; but he had not yet been in an ocean storm.

"The ship's steady now; but you'll find before many days that she knows how to pitch and roll like a live thing."

Before sunset they were opposite Little Gull Reef, where the "Norman Monarch's" sister ship, loaded with a similar cargo, had grounded and gone to pieces only a few months before. By dark Montauk Light was made, and there the ship's course was laid for the far-away Straits of Gibraltar.

At home that night the father read from the evening paper, "Sailed this day from New Haven, steamship 'Norman Monarch,' Capt. Duncomb, for Constantinople." And that was the last word from the "Norman Monarch" for many a day. She was out somewhere among the fogs and the rain and the winds, somewhere in the great Atlantic, pushing slowly across, through sunshine and storm, towards the Mediterranean.

CHAPTER III.

ON THE OCEAN.

No one on shore could know anything about it, but in truth they were having a wild time of it out there in the Atlantic.

The third night from port shut down black and threatening. When the steward came on deck to close the cabin skylights, the captain ordered,

"Jim, get out a spare canvas and cover the glass. Make all snug."

"Ay, ay, sir."

And when Jim thought his work was done, the captain, looking it over, said,

"That wont do; get another line around and stow the canvas tighter," and then to Harry,

"You've no idea, my hearty, what a bit of wind can do if its fingers once get a fair hold. It can handle the water pretty well, slippery as 't is; but if I'd give it half a chance to-night, you'd see it strip the main sheet to ribbons, or if that held, get mad and take the mast overboard. That'll do, Jim. See that all's fast below."

Harry and Will turned in early. The captain

prepared for a night on deck. The wind increased steadily, and the ship pitched and rolled and rose and sank so that there was no keeping in one's bunk but by holding on. Of course there was no sleeping.

"Cousin Will, shut up down here, and remembering what the captain said, I can't help thinking the wind is a great giant outside, with big arms that are picking up the waves and making hammers of them, with the ship for the anvil and us inside of it."

"Yes, only an anvil isn't alive, and you'd think the ship was. I fancy your giant is Neptune, and we are one of his harnessed horses that wont drive. I hope he wont thrash much harder."

Suddenly there was a staggering blow that nearly pitched them to the floor, then a rush not of one giant, but as though of a thousand feet along the deck, a crash of glass, a great surge of water through the cabin. They sprang down, holding by their berths. The state-room floor was ankle-deep. Just then the ship rolled their way. In an instant they were drenched from head to foot through the open door.

One of the cabin tables broke loose and began splitting into bits whatever it could reach. The steward worked his way in and hunted it with ropes as though it was a wild beast. Will and

Harry joined in it of necessity. It was worse than a bull-fight. A beast they could have shot, but this they could only lasso and tie.

The table was secured. The water drained away into the hold. They wrapped themselves as well they could in blankets and climbed back to bed.

"Harry, do you know what all that meant?"

"No, Cousin Will."

"We 'shipped a sea'—a heavy one. I don't know how many such the 'Norman Monarch,' with her heavy freight, could stand. We are 'lying to,' facing the storm. A wave covered the bows of the ship as she pitched into it. As they lifted, the water raced the length of the deck. What damage it did there, there is no knowing. It would be an easy thing for it to break a man's bones or to kill him. Except for the canvas over the skylight we might have had enough in here to have knocked us down and drowned us."

The ship was riding easier. Tired out, after a time they were half asleep. Suddenly with a shriek Harry sat straight up in his bed—and a sorry-looking figure he was, haggard and wet and wrapped in blankets—but a laugh was ready, though with a good deal of disgust in it, by the time his eyes were open. A pair of fat ship-rats, disturbed by the water, had pattered across his face and shoulders. He saw them now scurrying away through the cabin with more of their kind, and a boot after them from Will's bunk underneath.

Then they dozed off again. It seemed strange to Will that it should be so with such surroundings and interruptions, but through it all, over and over in his mind ran the refrain,

> "Rocked in the cradle of the deep
> I lay me down in peace to sleep;
> Secure I rest upon the wave,
> For thou, O Lord, hast power to save.
> I know thou wilt not slight my call,
> For thou dost mark the sparrow's fall,
> And calm and peaceful is my sleep,
> Rocked in the cradle of the deep."

Presently they both were sound asleep. With the sunrise the wind died still more away. By noon it was a dead calm, but it was colder and the still clouds looked thick and soft.

As Will and Harry sat lounging on the deck, quietly the snow began to fall. Faster and faster it came; there was scarcely any motion of the ship, only a lazy roll, for the machinery had stopped for cleaning and oiling; faster and faster, softly, until deck and spars and shrouds were thick with it, and then the clouds parted and down through it all came the sunlight. It was very beautiful.

"Look at this, and then think of last night. Could there be a greater contrast?" said Will. "It is fairy-like. I'll tell you, Harry, I must write something for Nellie about this, to go in the first home letter."

What Nellie received weeks later, when the first letters came, was this:

THE SNOW-FALL.

Gently the snowflakes are falling,
    A pure and a beautiful band,
Floating in numberless millions
    From some far-away spirit-land.

Surely the flakes must be fairies;
    We think they are nothing but snow,
Yet they are dancing the dances
    Of fairyland down here below.

Dwelling for ever in gladness,
    In palaces flashing with light,
They saw our ship sailing the ocean,
    And thought they would robe it in white.

Changing their forms as by magic,
    They leaped from their bright abode;
Caught by the elves of the wild wind,
    On elfin cars downward they rode.

Ceased is the fall of the fairies,
    And safe from their journey on high,
Now in the sunlight they're smiling
    At fairy friends up in the sky.

Pining for home are the fairies;
    The space they must traverse is long,
But by magic again, they vanish;—
    Up bridges of sunshine they're gone.

Later there came a morning when the captain took Harry up to the bridge, and pointing away off to the west, said,

"Look there, my lad, what do you see?"

"A dim something like a great whale-shaped cloud low down on the water. Is it land, captain?

"It's just that, my hearty; and a pretty bit of land it is, rising right up in mid-ocean. It's one of the Azores. Many a time I've run in there for shelter in rough weather. I'd have done it the other day if we'd been nigh enough. This one's Flores. It's a nice name. It means the 'Island of Flowers.' It lies right in our course. It makes no odds whether I sail to the north or to the south of it. I'll go to the south. It's safe enough in this weather. I'll keep close in shore and give you a chance to rest your eyes with a sight of green hills. You look a mite peaked. Well, it has been pretty tough weather for landsmen. I'd like to give you a run ashore, but I can't do that till we make Gibraltar, but I'll give you a good look, my boy."

"Thank you, captain."

And very pleasant it was for the travellers to look out from their ship at the picturesque Azores as they sailed among them past Flores, the largest of them, and Pico and St. George with its mountain 3,500 feet high, wearing its vapor cap as they sailed under it. "It's majesty seldom doffs it," the captain told them, no matter who is passing. Once there was a sharp flurry of excitement when the lookout reported from the mast-head a wreck in sight.

"Where away?" shouted the captain, as he sprang to the bridge and swept the rough water with his glass.

The dismantled hulk, rigged with a jury mast, was drifting off to leeward.

"Hard aport!" the captain called to the helmsman when he saw it; and after a minute, "Steady, so."

They ran down to the wreck, close alongside, but there was no sign of life and no flag set. Plainly it was deserted.

Past island after island they sailed, in and out, until all were astern—only the wild ocean in sight and the wild clouds overhead. Then again the course was laid for Gibraltar.

CHAPTER IV.

ACROSS THE ATLANTIC.

But for more than a month no word came to the waiting home friends of what was going on out there on the ocean. Then one glad day the first little white sheet reached the mother. It was a ray of sunlight to her, more welcome than real sunshine is after rain and cold. Harry wrote:

"Straits of Gibraltar, March 29.

"Dear Folks: I half like the ocean and half do n't. I was glad enough last night when the captain came to the cabin door, after I had gone to bed, and shouted down, 'Where are you, my boy? What! turned in so early! There's something outside you'd want to see.'

"'What is it?' I asked.

"'Not much. Only the Point St. Vincent Light, to tell you you're across the pond.'

"In about two minutes I was on deck, standing with the captain by the port railing.

"Where is it?" I asked him.

"'Watch a bit over there to port,' he said, 'and you'll see it. It's a revolving light; shows only every two minutes or so.'

"In a minute there it was, away off to the north, shining like a star, as bright as Venus, which was shining beautifully, low down over our stern.

"I liked the ocean then; and now I like it more, and feel better. Just now we are in the Straits of Gibraltar; we are rushing through them almost like a race-horse. There's a strong wind astern that makes the waves race with us and caps them with white; and long strips of green and blue water are all about us, under a sky where the clouds are racing too. And along the shore there are strips of brighter green. They look just like fresh, grassy meadows, but they are only shallow water. And there is a great white ship coming towards us, like a pile of snow, and the Stars and Stripes are flying from the peak. Spain is close on one side and Africa on the other. The great, wild ocean is behind us, and right ahead is Gibraltar, where we will anchor to-night and will land to-morrow, if all goes well and the captain does not land us instead on an ugly reef ahead, where he left one of his ships a few years ago; or on Diamond Rock, where a flagship of the English navy once went aground.

"It is all very fine now, and now I am feeling strong and happy enough to fly. But haven't there been days when I felt just the opposite?—

like the boy the captain tells about. The boy was seasick, and the captain wanted him to come on deck, thinking the fresh air would do him good; but he could n't get him to stir out of his bunk. So one day he thought he would make sure of it. He rushed down to the cabin, shouting, 'Quick, quick! tumble on deck; the ship's going to sink!' And the seasick fellow answered very deliberately, 'I'm glad of it. I hope she will.'

"I have n't been quite as bad as that, but I was seasick enough to be real homesick. I said to the captain it was a fib he told that boy, and he ought n't to have done it; but he ha-ha-ha'd—
"'T was n't, neither. I said the ship was going to sink; and so she was—into the trough of the sea—' which was not what he said.

"I'm not homesick now; but would n't I be even gladder than I am if I could just take a big jump to you all for a few minutes, and then back here again.

"Cousin Will is going to write some more.
"Good-by,
"HARRY HOWARD."

And Will wrote by the same mail:

"Dear Uncle: The first part of our voyage is accomplished without mishap. There have been stormy days, but not many of them. The third night out was the worst. The wind then was very heavy; the waves swept the deck and flooded the cabin; but, as a whole, and for the month of March, the voyage has been a remarkably favorable one. If the Mediterranean proves as friendly as was the Atlantic we shall be satisfied.

"We reached anchorage last night in the midst of heavy squalls of wind and rain. Harry would have been well pleased to have landed at once, after the quarantine officer had examined our papers; but we waited till this morning. Then we climbed over the side of the ship, and, watching our chance between the waves, dropped into one of the small boats lying alongside. The boatmen hoisted the long lateen sail, and we were off towards the great rock fortress.

"Gibraltar is more massive, steeper, lonelier, stronger than I had thought. Away up, 1,400 feet, the ridge cuts against the sky as sharp as a knife. On the further side, as we found afterwards, it is a sheer precipice; on this it slopes slightly, with terraces here and there, and woods and a town, down to the sea. The town, with its population of many nationalities, reaches some three miles, on the cliffs and under them, from the Europa Point Light at one end of the rock north to the other higher and steeper end, which faces Spain and is connected with the mainland by a flat strip of neutral territory. The cliffs are masked batteries; but we could see nothing of the cannon that we knew were there, thick enough to sweep every part of the harbor on which we were floating.

"We landed at the one public pier, hired a guide and donkeys, and proceeded to explore the 'Rock.' We went through long tunnels, dark and wet—so dark we could not see even our donkeys' ears. Here and there we came to little windowed chambers, like bright beads strung on a black thread, that gave beautiful glimpses past the muzzles of great guns, out over the water, towards Spain and the open Straits. Then we climbed higher. Harry had thought of Gibraltar as a smooth and bare rock. It is far from that. As we rode, all about us among the loose stones was a fine show of flowers, and lower down there were trees and thick shrubbery. We rode towards the Observatory on the high edge of the rock. As we came near it we knew that a few rods farther up the view beyond would open. One minute more, one step more, and there was the great Mediterranean, with dots over it that were ships, stretching away, hazy and blue, between classic lands to Malta and Cyprus, and at last to the Holy Land towards which Harry and I are journeying.

"We followed the ridge for a while, then rode along the face of the cliffs to the low southern end of the promontory, and so back through the town to the pier again.

"Dismounting there, we finished at once both our exploration of her Majesty's world-renowned fortress and our first donkey-ride. They are queer little beasts—these donkeys. They helped us to dismount at the last. Half way down the rock we came where an overflowed spring made quite a width of shallow water across the path. My donkey declined to go ahead, and Harry's sympathized. They set their innocent-looking little hoofs just at the edge of the water and quietly gazed across. The donkey-boys behind punched them with their sticks harder and harder, and lower and lower went the long ears pointing back at us. Just as Harry, who would as soon have thought of being thrown by a cow, reached out, laughing, to straighten the ears, up and out went the hind pair of heels like a flash of lightning, and instead of his ears Harry was clasping lower down tight around the donkey's chunky neck. My steed followed suit for a minute; then both were as meek as before—and as stubborn—looking dreamily across the water.

"The donkey-boys changed their tactics. Dropping their sticks, they came to close quarters, and bracing themselves behind, undertook to push the beasts ahead; but the donkeys braced themselves in front and pushed as hard back. Now it was simply a question of strength. If only they could be made to take a step and get their feet in the water, they would trot quietly through and go on as good as kittens. So both sides pushed harder and harder, and the donkeys found the boys were strongest, and thereupon, without the least warning, the two made a flying leap for the other side. Either of us could easily have sat a horse over a rail-fence, but in this case it was we who dropped into the water.

"At four o'clock we came off to the ship. Now I will send the letters ashore. It is nearly dark. Very soon we will be rounding the Point Europa Light, under way again for Constantinople.

"Yours sincerely,
"WILL HOWARD."

"P. S. The "Snow-fall" verses are for Nellie dear."

These letters were received, and read and reread, and then there was another long waiting while the "Norman Monarch" was pushing on again steadily through the Mediterranean towards her harbor in the Golden Horn.

CHAPTER V.

THROUGH THE MEDITERRANEAN.

On the fourth day from Gibraltar Harry and Will were sitting on deck reading when the captain came aft.

"Now, my hearties, we've had four days of still weather; 'bout time for another blow, is n't it?"

"Is a storm coming, captain?"

"Certainly. The glass says so; but I'd know it without that. Do you see the yellow look to the clouds yonder to windward? That's a sign of squalls. And higher up you see the waves in the gray clouds—not the broken ridges, they are no sign, but the smooth ones. They're a sure sign of rain. We must have all tight to-night." And the captain rolled forward.

"So we are likely," said Will, "to have Paul's experience of a storm in these waters. We are just about where he was wrecked on his way to Rome, for we are not far from Malta. You had better read the twenty-seventh chapter of Acts to-night, Harry."

That night the predicted storm came. It was

severe while it lasted. Such a storm would have wrecked the mariners who once sailed those waters in their round-hulled, oar-mounted, and star-guided triremes. It would surely have tested the sea-worthiness of Paul's stout ship; but the "Norman Monarch" shouldered her way through the waves so well that when the two days' storm was ended she had been delayed hardly more than an hour.

On the seventh day from Gibraltar a bold headland suddenly showed itself through the fog on the port bow. It was Cape Matapan, the southern point of Greece. After that came the pleasantest part of the whole voyage. The skies were clear; wind and waves were asleep. Their sailing was like a pleasant trip on some inland lake.

At midnight of the ninth day they neared the island of Tenedos. Will and Harry stood with the captain on the bridge while they sailed through the dangerous channel between the island and the mainland. The danger was from a covered rock lying directly in the way and unmarked by any buoy or light. Two men were at the wheel.

The moon was bright overhead. Two or three lighthouses shone like stars on the horizon. A soft land-breeze brought off odors from the damp pine forests of Asia. Harry was leaning against the rail. Will was thinking back to the day before the fall of Old Troy, when the main body of the Greeks withdrew to this island, leaving behind them, before the walls of Troy, the fatal wooden horse filled with their warriors.

The captain was alert, watchful. He knew that here was the most dangerous place in the whole voyage. If the weather had been rough he would not have dared risk the passage. He would have taken the longer route outside the islands. But now all was very still and beautiful, hushed, as though asleep.

Suddenly, clear and sharp, rang out, "Port your helm!"

"Port it is, sir."

Then silence, while the ship's bows swung off slowly to the east.

"Steady!"

"Steady, sir." And the wheel whirled as the men let go their hold upon it and it yielded to the strain of the rudder. Silence again, while the captain puffed fiercely at his pipe.

"Starboard!"

"Starboard it is, sir."

And in a minute again, "*Hard a starboard! Hard!*"

"Hard it is, sir."

"Hold her!"

"Ay, ay, sir." And the ship swept in a short curve swiftly towards the north.

"Steady!"

"Steady, sir." And the chains rattled again over the whirling wheel.

"How does she point?"

"Nor'-nor'east, sir."

"Keep her so for half an hour." And the captain knocked the ashes out of his pipe, gave orders when he was to be called, told his passengers good night, and turned in for a cat-nap, leaving the first mate in charge.

Harry and Will turned in also, and slept soundly for a few hours; but they were called again before sunrise. As they came on deck the ship was just entering the Dardanelles. They passed close under the steep and high banks of the European side, with the hills of Asia two or three miles away on the right. From behind one of those hills the sun rose with a fine show of red; but before it was fairly up the clouds hid it again.

Then came the first view of a Turkish town, with picturesque minarets tipped with black, and domed mosques and red-roofed, low, gray houses, and ruined fortifications.

Nearly opposite, on the Asiatic side, was Charnak. This was the quarantine station, and the ship "lay to" while the health officers were examining her papers.

Farther north they passed where a long, fortified point of Asia almost lapped the higher shore of Europe in front of them.

"It must have been near here," said Will, "that Xerxes and Alexander bridged the Hellespont (that was its old name), and crossed their immense armies. And, according to the stories, it was here also that Leander tried to swim across and failed, and that Lord Byron tried and succeeded."

"It does n't look far," said Harry, "for a good swimmer. I believe I could do it myself in fair weather."

"The width in the narrowest part is less than a mile," replied Will. "No doubt it has been crossed many times by good but untitled swimmers."

They sailed for fifty miles through the Dardanelles to the northern entrance, then swept past Gallipoli with its rocky bluff and lighthouse, and steamed out into the Sea of Marmora.

By this time the bright morning had settled into a stormy day. As they sailed north it was through rough water and under a beating rainstorm that drove the travellers below decks and kept them there till night.

But late that night, although the rain continued, they were up again and on the bridge with the captain, where he stood watchful and a little anxious, for somewhere close before them in the foggy darkness lay the land and Constantinople. It was too bad a night to make the inner harbor. He must find anchorage in the open roadway outside.

"Half speed!" came the order. "Cast the lead! Slow her!"

"Cast the lead. Slow her again!"

"Cast the lead! *Stop her!* DOWN WITH THE ANCHOR!"

Rattle and plunge went the chains, and just in time the ship swung to, safe for the night, close off the San Stefano Light.

Through what remained of the night Will and Harry slept soundly; but by sunrise they were on deck again, eager for the first view of the great city.

And there before them could be plainly seen now Constantinople; not glittering, as it so often does, in splendid sunlight, but dim under a drizzling rain, with old walls at the water's edge, with towers and domes and minarets, with black cypresses marking where there were once graves, with crowds and crowds of poor houses.

The anchor was hoisted. The ship gained

headway. A pilot hailed them. They took him on board, passed close around Seraglio Point into the Bosphorus and the inner harbor, steamed for a few minutes longer carefully among a swarm of sailing vessels and steamboats and lighters and ships' boats and swift, duck-like caiques; then the quick order was given, "Let go!" The anchor plunged; the chain whirled for a moment over the smoking windlass. The voyage was ended, and they were safely moored in the Golden Horn.

CHAPTER VI.

CONSTANTINOPLE.

Harry was eager to land. The two shawl-straps and the hand-bags were packed. That was all their baggage. There were plenty of caiques flitting about over the water. One was hailed and was alongside in a moment.

"Good-by, captain."

"Good-by, my hearty, and good luck to you. Good-by, Mr. William. Step quick from the ladder, and sit right down in the bottom of the boat. Those caiques are good for their work, but they wont bear any deck cargo. They're too light on the water for that. Good-by, again. The ship'll miss you on the home voyage."

As they swung down the rope-ladder it was with hearty respect that they bumped against the black sides of the good ship that had brought them safely seven thousand miles, to the end of their voyage and to the shelter of the finest harbor in Eastern waters.

The ladder swung with their weight. Harry glanced down rather doubtfully at the caique waiting to receive them.

"A queer boat," he remarked meditatively; "as queer as its name; shaped like the half of an Indian club, and with its bows at the wrong end."

"Let me advise you, Harry: don't touch it anywhere but as far down inside as you can suddenly get. Subside in it, as you would into a birch canoe, else, Harry, it will suddenly seem to you queerer still."

They embarked safely, and disembarked without mishap, only a few strokes away, at the stone front of the "Artillery Yard" on the northern side of the harbor—the Gàlata side. The boatman was dismissed, satisfied with a few pieces of depreciated paper currency.

The inclosure where they had landed was large, with piles of war material over it, and groups of soldiers working lazily. To the left, outside, lay the carcass of a dead horse; and about it, crouching on piles of dirt, walking slowly and sleepily about, lying in the sun, were crowds of dogs.

"Cousin Will, are those miserable, yellow, sleepy curs the noted 'dogs of Constantinople' that I expected to be half afraid of, lest I should get in their way or step on them and be bitten or barked at to pay for it?"

"Yes, those are a pack of the noted dogs. They are waiting there till night comes, when they will save the city authorities the trouble of burying the dead horse. They are good for scavengers, and for nothing else. You will see their like everywhere, dull, cowardly fellows, sneaking across one's path in the daytime, or curled up asleep under foot—that way all day, but noisy enough and active enough at night."

They passed out of the arsenal yard, and at once were in one of the narrow, crowded, dirty, but thoroughly interesting streets of the city. It was easier walking in the roadway than to try to keep the narrow sidewalk. But walk where they would, they had to avoid pools of mud and sleepy dogs, and horses and donkeys, and porters carrying on their shoulders loads larger than themselves, and crowds of men of all nationalities, and women veiled with white lace so drawn about their heads and faces and bodies as to look to Harry like shrouded corpses afoot.

Strange enough these Oriental streets appeared in contrast with the very different Western life which the travellers had left behind them.

Half an hour or so after leaving the ship they had crossed the "Artillery Yard," had passed the gate unchallenged, had walked the length of the street running west under the heights of Pera, and were standing waiting at the toll-gate of the great floating bridge across the Golden Horn—

the bridge which connects Old and New Constantinople, Stamboul and Gàlata.

Said Will, "I doubt, Harry, if ever before two individuals of our nationality entered Turkey as unnoticed as we have been—not anywhere a sign of a Custom-House officer!"

"Isn't it just possible it was an oversight?"

"Well, it may have been; we wont complain. But we gave them every opportunity. We came away in broad daylight, with our luggage in our hands. We did everything but wait; and as for waiting, they could not have expected that as a voluntary thing from any living Yankee—certainly not from two!"

The place at which they now stood is the best point for general observation in all Constantinople. One cannot overlook the whole city from it; he can see only that which lies on the near sides of the hills that rise all along the Golden Horn; but the advantage is that a large part of the city is sure to come to him—so constant is the current of humanity back and forth along the bridge.

They spent a good part of the day there, as it was, and might easily have spent the whole without tiring.

"Harry," asked Will, "how would you describe what we are looking at now—this constantly changing scene?"

Harry immediately set his active imagination to work, and replied, "It is a huge kaleidoscope."

"Good."

"It is a gorgeous flower-garden—poppies, sunflowers, hollyhocks, everything—and with all the flowers in procession, back and forth, marching as steadily as the waters flow underneath."

"Rather fanciful, but less overdrawn than some might think."

"What would you say about it, Cousin Will?"

"I? I don't know. That it is an allegory of life, comic and serious, restless, changing, unsatisfied. Or how would this do? It is a new version of Tennyson's 'Brook,' where the men that come and the men that go, instead of English rustics, are people of every nationality under the sun, dressed in all the colors of the rainbow; and where the stream 'that hurries down by thirty hills, and still goes on and on for ever,' isn't at all 'Philip's brook,' but the 'sweet waters' of the Golden Horn."

"But, Cousin Will, isn't that rather more fanciful than mine was?"

"Well, no matter, so long as both fancies are true. In the East one expects to be imaginative."

It was certainly a most picturesque crowd that was passing before them.

"There comes a party of fine-looking fellows. Do you know what they are, Cousin Will?"

"Do you see they are armed and have rows of little pockets filled with cartridges across the breasts of their brown, close-fitting coats? They belong to the Circassian tribes. Such as they are the most turbulent and lawless men in Constantinople. A few months ago a band of them surrounded a man on one of these bridges, robbed him, and then went their way unmolested."

"At night?"

"No; in broad day. But the times are quieter now, and there is no danger from them. There are some Greeks. They belong to another fine-looking race. Notice how becoming their dress is. The jacket and rich silk undervest and sash and loose trousers and silk stockings, all in plain neutral colors, are in excellent taste. And there are Persians, with conical felt-hats and long, flowing robes; and priests, with green turbans and white and fur-lined cloaks. All these are the more noticeable because of the plainness of their dress among the brilliant costumes about them; just as at home, in our black-dressed and gray-dressed crowds, we would very quickly notice a man dressed, for instance, like that one, in a red fez and blue jacket and crimson vest and white trousers, with bare legs, and yellow, pointed shoes. Here, you see, the rule is colors and combinations such as those. The plainer colors are the exception."

"I believe I could watch this river or flower-garden or kaleidoscope or menagerie or circus, or whatever it is, all day without growing tired," said Harry.

"Yes, and you would see something new and Oriental at almost every moment. Harry, do you remember that painting at home of the 'Derby Day' in England by C. Green?"

"Yes; a fine picture."

"Well, I wish an equally skilful artist would strike for fame with 'Midday on the Stamboul Bridge.' The material is here. If he did his part he would wake and find himself famous. The landscape portion of such a painting would be hardly less interesting than the main subject. The middle distance would include, just at the end of the bridge, the large 'New Mosque,' so called, not because it is new now, but was once, when it took its name, some hundreds of years ago. Then beyond, for the background, the land slopes from the water, and shows here and there all over it among rough buildings white minarets as slim as fingers, pointing above the domes of their mosques; and black cypresses that are almost equally slim growing singly or in groups, and that not merely seem like black-uniformed sentinels, but are that; they are faithful long-lived sentinels over the dead. Each tree marks a place of burial, although often now, after the long years, no signs of the grave remain. Off to the left the land ends in Seraglio Point, pointing towards the heights of Scutari across the Bosphorus, and washed on the further side by the waves of the Sea of Marmora, and rough waves they are when the wind is in the south.

"Seraglio Point was the earliest settled part of this old and storied city. Strange things and wonderful it has looked upon. One of the most thrilling times of all must have been no more than about four hundred years ago, when the Christians still held the city, but were fighting their last battles against the besieging Turks under Mohammed II.

"There was some hope of final victory for the besieged, provided an expected Genoese fleet, with a supply of food and of soldiers, should arrive in time; and provided, further, that when it arrived it should dare to do so rash a thing as attack the strong Turkish fleet which was blockading the harbor.

"The Genoese ships hove in sight. The whole city could see them as far off as the horizon on the Sea of Marmora. There were but five ships, while the Turks had three hundred, though many of theirs must have been very small. It seemed unlikely that the allies would do anything but come near enough to see their danger, and then turn about and sail away as fast as wind and oar could take them. But when they neared the port still they kept on, as though they were blind or foolhardy. A few of the Turkish ships may have been concealed around the Point, but most of them were in plain sight, curved across the mouth of the Bosphorus in order of battle.

"The Genoese were not blind; they were heroes worthy of the records of their race. They struck the Turkish fleet close by the crowded walls of the city. They fought their way back and forth through it with Greek fire, with discharges of artillery, with hand-to-hand grappling and fighting, with crushing blows from their beaked prows.

"The Turkish captains knew that Mohammed was watching it all from the shore, and that he was likely to hold them responsible for defeat with their lives. Of course they fought desperately. But it was useless. Their entire fleet was scattered up and down the shores of the Bosphorus. The Genoese anchored safely inside the chain that protected the mouth of the Golden Horn. For the time the city was safe.

"But, Harry, we have spent a good part of the day here already; it's time for us to be moving."

"A little longer, Cousin Will. Just see what a brilliant show those soldiers make."

"Yes, the Sultan keeps his army well equipped, whatever else he neglects. That officer on his splendid black horse has gold enough over his white uniform to make a fortune for the poverty-stricken wretches that he is almost running down.

"And there, I suppose, is one of the Sultan's carriages, English built, with white driver and footman, and in the seat of honor a fine-looking negro in plain modern dress. He holds a place of great trust in the royal household."

"And what a contrast," said Harry, "in that half-naked beggar behind, carrying what looks as much like a stuffed pig as anything, with its head and ears cut off."

"It is a leather bottle of water, Harry. The man is so emaciated and so scantily clothed very likely he is some pilgrim devotee. Now, as he comes up to us, though we cannot understand him, perhaps he is doing what it is like them to do—offering us a drink of water in exchange for our prayers for the well-being of his soul. You will see that kind of bottle everywhere, here and in Palestine, carried about the streets by men and

WATER-CARRIER, WITH SKIN BOTTLE.

by donkeys, sometimes with water for drink and sometimes for sprinkling the streets."

"I suppose," said Harry, "I might come to drink out of them, but I'd have to be half-famished first."

"Well, if we must go on we must; but let's not hurry."

They paid a bit of paper money at the toll-gate, then strolled leisurely along the bridge, past venders of fruit of many kinds (best of all, luscious egg-shaped oranges of Jaffa), past groups of men, past black steamboats that make the bridge a station in their frequent trips up and down the Bosphorus, across the long bridge, into Old Constantinople.

It was growing late when they came to a quiet hillside street among the crooked streets of Stamboul. Presently they stopped before one of the most substantial and attractive public buildings in Constantinople, and one which is the centre of work that has been in the past, and is likely to be in the future, of vast benefit to Turkey. The building is the "Bible House," the busy hive belonging to the American Board of Commissioners for Foreign Missions. After the long voyage, and after the strangeness and tumult of the crowded streets, the travellers gladly entered the quiet building. They inquired of the janitor for Doctor Wood. They were directed to his room on the second floor, but the door was locked. They passed from door to door marked with the familiar and honored names. Every door was closed. No one was at work. Was it a holiday?

But at last they were directed to a corner room in an upper story. They lifted the latch there, and, opening the door, found themselves suddenly no longer among a strange people, and no longer with the feeling that there were thousands of miles between them and anything home-like. They were among friends and at home. They were in the midst of a Christian prayer-meeting. It was a most welcome surprise to them and a pleasant introduction to the noble missionaries of Constantinople.

When at last it was time for the travellers to take their leave the venerable Doctor Wood said to Will,

"Now, Mr. Howard, you and your young friend must make my house in Scutari your home while you remain in this part of the world. You will be among friends there, and from there it will be easy to make such excursions as you may wish through the city and up and down the Bosphorus."

Certainly, after their rough voyage, nothing could be pleasanter than to be received into such a harbor. They very gladly accepted the invitation.

That evening Will and Harry were most kindly welcomed at the modest and beautiful home on the heights of Scutari. And the kindness of the evening was only a sample of the attention that continued to be shown them during the whole of their stay in the neighborhood of Constantinople.

CHAPTER VII.

ST. SOPHIA.

Doctor Wood said at the breakfast-table, "Mr. Howard, are you and Master Harry inclined to walk this morning or to rest?"

"To walk, sir. It is not walking that we are tired of, but sailing. So where had we better go to-day?"

"You might visit the Mosque of St. Sophia, or the old walls with the 'Seven Towers.' On Friday, if you like, I will go with you to see the 'Howling Dervishes.'"

"Then to-day we will go to St. Sophia. There is nothing in Constantinople I am more interested in than that."

"If you can gain admittance, it will be well for you to be there about noon."

When Will and Harry had crossed in the little ferry steamer to Stamboul (Old Constantinople), and were walking through the streets towards St. Sophia, Harry asked,

"If St. Sophia is a mosque, why is it named as though it was a Christian church? Why has n't it a Mohammedan name?"

Cousin Will answered, "It has a Mohammedan name which is sometimes used. But the original St. Sophia was built and named by a Christian emperor, by Constantine the Great, away back in the beginning of the fourth century. The first church was of wood, and was more than once burned down or pulled down before the present splendid temple of brick and stone was built on the same site, two hundred years later, by the Emperor Justinian. In the Middle Ages it was one of the richest and most sacred of all the Christian churches. But when the Turks came in the fifteenth century, and after terrible fighting won the city walls, everything was changed. The Turkish commander was Mohammed II. He marched his troops through these streets to the front of the church. Then he entered where, in a few minutes, we too will enter. Only he rode in on horseback, tradition says, with all his train; and instead of being peaceably inclined, as we are, when he found a vast crowd collected there of frightened women and children and old men, he slew them all or made captives of them. Those were fearful days in Constantinople. Ever since that time St. Sophia has been a Mohammedan mosque."

Now they had reached the courtyard of the great building.

"See," said Will, "what a huge, irregular pile of brick and stone it is. From the outside it looks as though there was no plan or order about it, with its many domes and half-domes and minarets against the sky. But we will find what it is inside, underneath these domes—that is, if we can get in. Come on, and we will try."

At the heavily-curtained outer entrance they were met and stopped by one of the priests of the mosque.

"Have you a permit?" he demanded.

"No, we have none."

"Then it is against the rules to admit you."

"But suppose we pay you, instead of paying for a permit?"

"For twenty piasters* apiece you may come with me."

"Very good; we will pay you forty piasters."

Then the curtain was swung aside and they were admitted; but they had no more than crossed the threshold before they were checked sharply. They must remove their shoes, and then go on in their stocking-feet, or else make choice from among the light, heelless slippers that were spread beside the door. Neither alternative was agreeable.

"The slippers are a deal too big," said Har-

* About one dollar.

ry, "but I suppose they are better than nothing."

They chose the slippers, and went forward with their guide.

"Is this the church?" asked Harry of Cousin Will.

"No, though it might well be for its beauty and its size. It is a kind of great vestibule inclosing the inner church. Much of it is covered now with bright stucco over the old frescos and mosaics of the Christian time. The rest is polished marble; and the floor, you see, is rich marble mosaic. The guide says they are engaged now in the church in the mid-day worship, and he asks us to go into the galleries first. There we can see the interior and the worshippers without disturbing the service."

As they followed the guide, Harry exclaimed in astonishment,

"Why, I expected to find stairs into the gallery, and this, where he is leading us, is more like an up-hill wagon-road!"

"Nothing could give us a better idea," said Will, "of the thickness and massiveness of the different parts of the mosque. This passage-way winds up through the middle of the wall, doubling back and forth on itself, and yet is wide enough for three horsemen easily to ride abreast in it. If Mohammed rode his horse here he had room enough and to spare. And all the proportions of the great church are in keeping."

They came out into the lowest of the broad galleries, and from it looked far down to the floor and far off and up, past clusters of columns and arches and lesser domes, towards the one wonderful dome flattened to the slightest possible curve, in imitation of the curve of the distant sky, which crowns and beautifies the whole.

Harry looked and looked, and at last exclaimed, "How immense it is!" and then after a moment, "and how beautiful it is!"

And Will added, "There is nothing like it in all the world—269 feet long, 243 wide, 180 high! Polished stone-work everywhere!—107 stone columns of many colors, brought for their beauty from Egypt, from Ephesus, from Baalbec, from Rome. There are mosaic floors, partly covered with rich Turkish carpets. On the walls are gold mosaics and Mohammedan symbols and passages from the Koran and abundance of stucco-work, covering what were once, in the old days, fair pictures of saints and angels and of Christ. Indeed, the sight of all is something to thrill one! Your adjectives were right, Harry; 'immense' and 'beautiful' it certainly is."

They stood for a long time in the gallery. A

monotonous chanting filled the place. Looking down upon the lines of men on the pavement below, they could see them bowing and stooping with their foreheads to the ground, worshipping towards Mecca. They noticed that these lines of worshippers reached diagonally across the floor, instead of at right angles with the walls. It reminded them again that the church had not been built for the convenience of Mohammedan devotees. It does not lie four-square towards their sacred city.

When the service was ended and the greater part of the company had gone away, they went down from the gallery and entered the body of the mosque. There they wandered among columns and arches and stone fountains and praying places and chapels and pulpits. Many as they are, they give no slightest effect of crowding, so great is the space between the walls. The guide had seemed inclined to lead them only around the sides of the church in the shelter of the galleries. At last Will asked, "Would we be allowed to walk across the carpeted floor directly under the central dome?"

The guide hesitated a moment, but answered, "Yes, if you would pass along without much stopping, so as not to attract attention. But only a few years ago such a thing could not have been.

In fact, then you would not have been allowed here at all. If you had tried to get in you would have been killed; and there are plenty who would have you out now if they dared to touch you."

They walked quietly to the centre of the church, and standing there looked straight up between the surrounding columns and arches and half-arches that narrowed above them, up to the sky-like dome at the centre, one hundred and eighty feet from where they stood. As they looked down again Harry staggered for a moment. He was actually dizzy, the distances were so great and the proportions so perfect. That was the last. They passed on over the rich rugs, with glimpses between of the richer marbles underneath, to the entrance, exchanged there the slippers for their own shoes, dismissed the attendants, and came from what seemed like an inner world, weird and mysterious and old, into the other noisy and crowded world outside.

CHAPTER VIII.

DERVISHES.

THE Howling and the Whirling Dervishes! Who would imagine that anywhere in the world there could be men with forms of religion and of worship such as theirs!

In one of Will's frequent home letters he described the visit which they made with Doctor Wood to the establishment of some of these strange people. He wrote:

"We are just back from visiting the Howling Dervishes. We reached their place after a long walk with Doctor Wood through narrow streets and then past a very large Moslem Cemetery, dark under its many cypress-trees and unique with its strangely figured and painted tombstones. There was a small courtyard, then an entrance hall where we exchanged our shoes for slippers, and beyond that the main room of the mosque. There we found seats outside of a railing under the galleries. The central part of the room inclosed by this railing was some forty feet square. At one side was a small shrine looking towards Mecca, and on the walls were hung iron scourges and knives and long rods, which were once used by the Dervishes as instruments of torture, and doubtless they would still be so used had not the Government of late forbidden it. Presently a company of men gathered in the inclosure, and seated themselves on mats in a line reaching half way around the room. Most of them were in their ordinary working dresses. There were several soldiers in uniform and a number of negroes. Many looked like day-laborers and tradesmen. Besides these there were a number of priests—a chief priest and his attendants.

"These were the Howling Dervishes. The service commenced with prayer and responsive chanting and bowing of themselves, much after the ordinary style of Mohammedan worship. This continued with increasing earnestness for about forty minutes. Then came the second part of the service. They all rose and stood in a long line shoulder to shoulder around the inclosure. The rugs were removed excepting a few that were placed in front of the line for the use of a number of old men who were to sit and act as leaders in the chanting and howling which followed.

"Then they began, quite moderately at first, howling softly together and swaying themselves slightly—sidewise, forward, backward, forward, sidewise—in perfect time with their voices. But the howling increased and the swaying increased. The old men beat their hands faster and faster. The excitement seemed contagious, until at last the action was violent. The line swayed rapidly back and forth, far towards the left, back to the right, forward almost to the ground—faster, faster! And the howls! They were given with the full force of the men's lungs. It seemed impossible that this could continue for many minutes, but they kept it up without a break for a full hour. Now and then some would show signs of oppression from the heat. Thereupon the attendant priests would step forward with their white caps and white robes, which the men would take in exchange for their thick fezes and outer garments, until a good part of the line came to be dressed in white. The transfers were made with no pause in the howling and swaying.

"At the end of the hour the voices were beginning to fail. A few had to fall out of the line and stagger from the room. Gradually the howl became scarcely more than a loud panting. Now the motion was varied slightly, but was still violent—a rising on the toes and heavy settling again, and the sidewise swaying. With some this came to be seemingly mechanical, just an involuntary violent jerking of the muscles. It lasted a quarter of an hour longer, making the whole time after the introductory service an hour and a quarter. Then they rested. We thought they had finished, but, instead, they began all over again and went through with the same thing, only this time it had to be much shortened.

"After that the service changed. Flasks of water were brought and placed before the priest. He made gestures and signs over them, breathed on them, and blessed them. Then they were taken away. They were to be used as medicines.

"Nor was that the whole. A number of sick men now came forward to be healed. Their belief was that an evil spirit within them was tormenting them. In turn they touched the priest's hands with their lips and forehead, and then lay down at full length on the floor before him. The priest at once pressed his foot upon their shoulders, and then stood upon them for a moment with his full weight. The idea was to force out the evil spirit that caused the sickness. Then they rose, saluted the priest again, and withdrew.

"But neither was this the whole. They suppose that the priest is able not only to restore to health, but to insure continued health and an increase of strength. And so, after the sick men were gone, in came a troop of healthy-looking little children, three years old and over. In one group were six little girls. After kissing the priest's hands they lay down, side by side, before him. He walked deliberately over them, stepping from one to the other, then turned and walked back to his place. At the last a young man brought in a baby, possibly a year old, and seemingly sick. They laid it on the floor, with one man holding it by the feet and another by the shoulders, and then the old priest deliberately stepped on the child with his full weight, and stood there, just as he had on the grown men, only he appeared to be rather more careful now, stepping lightly and quickly, and steadying himself by the attendants at his side.

"That ended the service, excepting that there was to be something more of responsive prayer. We had seen and heard enough. As we withdrew we felt the need more than ever of the Christ-teaching for the little children and for the men and the women of these half-heathen lands."

To the same letter Harry added a few comments on another somewhat similar class of fanatics, the Whirling Dervishes. He wrote:

"Besides seeing those Howling Dervishes we have seen some whirling ones too; and odd enough they were! They wore high felt hats, with no rim, and a brownish dress that covered them from their necks to their heels. For a while they sat around the room like men; but then all at once they rose and changed into tops. The way they did it was this: they formed in line, turned themselves from brown to bright green by throwing off their outer dress, and marched a few times around the room. Then each one, as he passed in front of the shrine and priest, stretched out his arms and began whirling, moving at the same time slowly to his place on the floor.

"When the whole line had passed before the priest the entire floor was covered with them. They looked like open umbrellas, for they turned so fast their long, loose dresses flared out as though they were hooped. I timed the fastest one among them. He turned fifty-four times a minute; just think, almost once a second! It lasted for ten minutes. Then they rested, but almost right away commenced again. And so it kept on for an hour, when the spinning stopped and the service was ended.

"There has been so very, very much to write about, and I have not begun to have time enough for writing it all; and now we are nearly ready to travel on again towards Syria."

CHAPTER IX.

COAST OF ASIA MINOR.

THE day came for leaving Constantinople. They had engaged passage by the French line of steamships for Syria. The "Rio Grande," of that line, would carry them as far south as Smyrna; there they would change and take a coasting vessel for Beirût. They went on board their ship at four o'clock, and just as the sun was setting splendidly behind the city, and making the windows of Scutari blaze as though on fire, they sailed out from the Golden Horn and the Bosphorus into the Sea of Marmora.

The second evening brought them to Smyrna on the coast of Asia Minor; a busy city, with a fine harbor at the head of a mountain-encircled gulf—which gulf was all in a wild tumult as the ship entered it under the lashing of a fierce mountain storm.

The next morning Harry and Will landed, and roamed through the narrow streets and up to the ruins of an ancient castle on the top of a steep hill back of the city. While they were climbing the hill, in a lonely place, they heard shoutings behind them. They looked around, and there, close to them, and apparently chasing them, were four wild-looking Turks.

"Are they after us, Cousin Will?"

"I think not. But they are certainly very earnest about something," answered Will, and he quietly cocked his pocket revolver.

The shouting continued.

"Would they try to rob us?" Harry exclaimed, a little startled.

"It isn't likely, though they look equal to it, and the place could not be better chosen. More likely they want to force us to pay toll or to take them for guides to the castle. We will wait and find out."

The men came up, seemingly in great excitement. When they could make themselves understood it appeared that they were not robbers at all, but farmers. They had coins for sale.

In answer to Will's sign-questioning they said they had found the coins while digging in their fields. One of the men hastened away to bring them. There was a small bagful. They appeared to be genuine, and Will was glad to bargain for a few of them. Then they received from the "robbers" a very friendly good-by and went their way to the castle.

There they made a long stay, resting under

SMYRNA, PORT AND CASTLE.

the old walls and enjoying the grand view out over the city and gulf.

"I wish we had time," said Harry, "to go to the other side of these mountains to old Ephesus. We could do it, could n't we, if only the ship would wait a day?"

"Yes, we could easily go and return in a day, and have time to see the little that is left of the old grandeur that was there in the time of Paul and their great goddess Diana. Suppose we read now about Paul's work there;" and he turned to the 19th chapter of Acts, 23-41, in his pocket Testament.

They talked for a while longer about Ephesus; then Harry said,

"Cousin Will, I am in a hurry to be right in the very places the Bible tells about."

"You are in one of them now," replied Will. "This is one of the places which John names in Revelation. He was commanded to send his book to the church that is in Smyrna;* and he was told also to write certain encouraging words to 'the angel of the church that is in Smyrna.'† Here was one of the most important and prominent of all the early Christian communities. Very possibly the pastor to whom reference was made as the 'angel of the church' was Polycarp.

* Rev. 1:11.   † Rev. 2:8

And it was here, in the middle of the second century, that Polycarp was martyred.

"One of the early church Fathers gives a long account in Latin of the martyrdom as he had heard it described.

"He says that when Polycarp was brought to trial before the Roman officers he was urged to save himself by reviling Christ; but instead, he answered, 'Eighty and six years have I served Christ, and he never did me wrong; and how can I now blaspheme my King that has saved me? If you would know what I am, I tell you frankly, I am a Christian.' Then they brought him to the stake to be burned, and heaped the fuel about him and kindled the fire. Tradition says that when the fire was lighted, at first the flames would not touch their victim, but curved around him like an arch. Then a soldier pierced him through with his spear, and at that the blood flowed so as to put out the fire; and at the same time a dove flew from the wound, which some supposed was his soul escaping in that form to heaven. He was so saintly a man, and so closely associated with the apostle John and with the early interests of Christianity, that the church has always held him in reverence. The few writings of his which remain are of great value, especially in tracing the history of the books of the New Testament.

"Well, it is time to be moving towards the ship. Take one more look at the mountains, Harry, and the city and the gulf and the castle, for it is a fair picture, well worth remembering. Then we must go."

They were on board the ship "La Seine" when she sailed at sunset for her voyage along the coast of Asia Minor to Beirût.

CHAPTER X.

COAST OF SYRIA.

Harry and Will were on deck by daylight the next morning. They were sailing through beautiful scenery, close under bold spurs from the mainland of Asia Minor, in and out among islands, past dangerous-looking rocks.

In one place the ship swept around a rocky promontory whose height was crowned by a ruined castle with white, flat-roofed houses clustered beside it, and here and there among them the domes of mosques with their finger-like minarets pointing to the sky, and on the slope of the hill a dozen or so busy windmills. They sailed so near and so quickly, the pictures seemed like parts of a great panorama.

"I do n't want to leave all this and go below," said Harry, "but I'm too hungry to wait for the ten-o'clock breakfast. I'm going to try to get something to eat."

"You know how to ask for their regular morning meal?"

"Yes; if I say, 'Café,' they will bring me coffee and bread."

"You can send the waiter with mine on deck."

Harry went below to the cabin. After a rather long time he returned.

"Well," he said, "I had a funny time getting my breakfast."

"How was it?"

"I wanted the bread toasted, and I wanted a boiled egg. I made them understand about the bread by holding a piece of it over the hot coffee and pretending that it burned my fingers. But they couldn't make out at all at first what else I wanted."

"I thought I had told you their word for egg."

"You have, but they couldn't understand it. I suppose I mispronounced it. But I got the egg finally. I took a piece of paper and made a picture that looked something like a hen. Then I hurried (so they wouldn't think I wanted a chicken) and made an oval figure near the other. I showed it to them. They laughed, and in a minute brought me my boiled egg."

They sailed on, through scenery that was often grand and always beautiful, until late that afternoon, when they reached the island of Rhodes. A long point of sand, covered thickly with black and white windmills, hid the town as they approached. They rounded the point, and a little farther on cast anchor in front of the old towers of the Crusaders.

Lighters, some of them with freight and some empty for taking away freight, swarmed about the ship, and there were smaller boats for the passengers. The ship was anchored so far out there was no time for a visit to the shore. They had to be satisfied with a distant view of the ruined walls and of the narrow harbor entrance, once guarded by the great "Colossus of Rhodes," which was ranked as one of the seven wonders of the world, and with thinking and talking of the time, two thousand years before, when the place was rich and powerful and independent, and of the time, five hundred years before, when the Knights of St. John made it their home.

"Did not those knights have something to do with the history of Jerusalem?" asked Harry.

"Yes, the order originated in Jerusalem. It was in this way. A hospital was built there in the eleventh century for the use of the pilgrims to the Holy Sepulchre. Its nurses were called 'Brothers of St. John the Baptist, of Jerusalem.'

"In time this came to be a military as well as religious order, and the brethren were called 'Knights.' They became very rich and powerful, with establishments in all parts of Europe.

Their headquarters were at Jerusalem until the city was captured by Saladin in 1187. Afterwards they were in Acre, one of the places we are to visit on the coast of Syria, and then, in the early part of the fourteenth century, they came to Rhodes. They captured the island and fortified it—you can see the ruins of their castles—and held it against the Saracens for over two hundred years. There has been fierce fighting about these hills and waters that are so quiet now. We can hardly imagine it, more than we can that there have been terrible earthquakes here. Only sixteen years ago two thousand houses were destroyed by an earthquake.

"That lighter alongside appears to be the last, and it is nearly unloaded. We shall be under way again before dark. It is well we did not risk going on shore."

They sailed from Rhodes at five o'clock.

During a part of the next day—the second from Smyrna and the fourth from Constantinople—they were out of sight of land. On the fifth day they anchored for a few hours at Mercina. On the sixth they landed at Alexandretta, sailing again late in the afternoon. On the seventh day they passed Lattaque and Tripoli, and on the morning of the eighth day they approached Beirût. As they neared the anchorage the beautifully-located city covered the hills in front of them. To the right were other hills. To the left rose the peaks of Lebanon, capped apparently with white sand; but in fact the seeming sand was distant snow, covering peaks that were much higher than they looked in the clear atmosphere.

"Do you see that large stone building high up on the hills, just at the right of the city?" asked Will of Harry.

"Yes."

"It is the American Mission College. The work there and at Miss Everett's mission-school and home for girls, and in the Bible House, and in the Protestant church, and in the different first-class hospitals, is making Beirût the chief city for progress and influence in all Syria. It is now an active, prosperous city, and the people themselves say that the result is due chiefly to the influence of the Christians."

"But I wouldn't think it could have much trade with as poor a harbor as this is. I don't believe we could ever get ashore alive if there was much wind."

"Yet, poor as the harbor is," answered Will, "it is the best on the coast; and besides, it has the trade of Damascus. We shall find to-morrow a fine road—the only good one in all Syria—crossing the mountains between the two cities."

BEIRÛT.

By this time they had reached the anchorage. The engines were stopped. The captain's order, "Let go!" rang from the bridge. The chains rattled and the ship swung to her moorings.

With the letting go of the anchor another stage of their long journey was ended.

"Here come a crowd of boats with shouting boatmen all eager to take us ashore. Now, Harry, we will say good-by to the ship and let land travel take the place for a while of ocean travel."

They landed at the narrow stone pier, passed the Custom House without trouble, and were in the streets of Beirût.

The remainder of the day was spent in exploring the city and in preparing for the next day's journey across the mountains to Damascus.

CHAPTER XI.

BEIRÛT TO DAMASCUS.

"Come, wake up, wake up, Harry," called Cousin Will early the next morning.

"What time is it?" was the sleepy response.

"Three o'clock. Get up! You know to-day we begin our land travel in Syria."

In a minute Harry was out of bed. A good breakfast was ready for them of goat's milk, coffee and bread and butter, eggs and honey.

Then they went out into the quiet streets to find their way to the station of the diligence in which they had taken seats for their journey to Damascus. Their plan was to visit Damascus and Baalbec, and then return to Beirût. From Beirût Will expected to sail for Jaffa, though he hoped that some way would open in time by which they could make the whole journey by land.

"How still it is!" said Harry, as they walked, "and I would not have thought it could be so light as it is with only the stars shining; and how sweet the air is in some places! I suppose there are gardens on the other side of these high walls."

"Yes, and no doubt most beautiful ones. The

Oriental way is very different from ours—the opposite of ours. We share our flower-beds and lawns and courts with the passers on the street. Here they shut in everything as closely as possible."

"It seems selfish," said Harry.

"No, it is not that. The custom grew out of the need of high walls for protection. These regions are quiet now, but they have been wildly lawless at times."

"Do you know where you are, Cousin Will? I am all turned around. You are going down this street when I thought we ought to keep to the right."

"No, that would lead up to the Bible House and the mission church. I remember the way easily, so far, through the new part of the city. A little farther on, through the older streets and squares, it will be harder But if there is need we can inquire of some of these men that we meet with their loaded donkeys and camels."

"Seems to me they are moving early."

"Yes, but here, at this season, the night is more comfortable for travel than the day."

They asked the way once, to be sure they were right; and then, after a walk of twenty minutes through the streets of an Eastern city, they reached the diligence office.

The scene there was a strange one. In the dim light a crowd was gathering, men and women and children in Oriental dress, curious to see what travellers there were and to note all the preparations for the journey.

"It seems odd," said Harry, "to think that our talk and our dress must be as strange to them as theirs is to us. Is this the stage we are to take, all ready for the horses here in the yard?"

"Yes, that is the French diligence."

"Is it like those they use in Switzerland over the Alps?"

"Something like them. Here is the coupé in front under the driver's seat, and behind there is a second compartment, with the door opening to the rear. There is no 'middle interior,' and no 'banquette;' but in place of the banquette there is that covered place on top just behind the driver."

"I wish we could ride up there."

"We can as far as Sthorer."

"How far is that?"

"Half way. Another party has the seats engaged beyond."

There was slight delay; but at half-past four the passengers and baggage were in their places; the six horses were harnessed, three abreast; all was ready for the start. The driver and the guard climbed to their seat in front of Cousin Will and Harry. The horn sounded, and they were off. They drove rapidly through the city and across the open country beyond; past square, flat-roofed houses and pleasant gardens and high hedges of cactus and palm-trees and groves of umbrella-pines, all sweet and beautiful and strange in the fresh morning air, across the narrow strip of open country to the foot of the mountains. Then the long ascent of the Lebanon range began, gradual at first, but steeper and steeper for many miles.

"I never saw anywhere a better road than this," said Harry.

"It is a first-class road in every respect," replied Will, "and it is the same the whole way to Damascus. It is the only good road in all Syria. I wish its whole equipment was equally good. The wagons and coaches answer well enough, and some of the teams; but these harnesses! I am afraid of them.

"Do you see those patches of snow off to the left? It is what we thought was white sand as we saw it yesterday from the ship."

"Yes, and it is plainly enough snow, now that we are so nearly up on a level with it. How high would you think the mountains are?"

"They average about 7,000 feet, and nearly the whole range is the same as the part we are crossing now, just as wild and lonely and bare of trees and bushes. You know there are two lines of mountains that we are to pass to-day.

"To the east of this Lebanon range, and running parallel with it, is the lower, Anti-Lebanon range. Between them lies the long valley of Cœle-Syria.* Later we shall see, away off to the south at the end of the Anti-Lebanon range, the great snow-covered Mount Hermon. There are many references in the Bible to Hermon and Lebanon. One of the most beautiful is in the 133d Psalm.

"But Lebanon is mentioned oftenest, perhaps, in connection with its cedars. They were among the noblest of trees, and in the Bible imagery are often used to illustrate greatness and strength of character and exaltation and power. There are a few cedars found still among the bare mountains, but they are very few, compared with the forests that once flourished here; those, for example, from which Hiram supplied Solomon with wood for his buildings at Jerusalem. Instead of trees there is scarcely anything now but bare rock all about us."

"What sort of rock is it?" asked Harry.

"Limestone, most of it. It is a stone which is easily worked; so the makers of this road have

* "Hollow Syria."

had little trouble either in building the road or in keeping it in repair. There is certainly need of keeping it in good order, for we are meeting travellers over it all the time. There is another long train of covered wagons turning to one side to let us pass."

"Do you suppose the Government owns them?"

"No; they belong to the French company that have control of the road."

"I like to see these lines of camels," said Harry, "and the rough-looking men who are leading them, and the donkeys with loads as big as themselves; but I wonder why almost all of them keep to the rough side foot-path instead of taking the smooth road. Perhaps it cuts off some of the curves, or the road may be too hard and smooth for them. I should think that the camel's big padded feet, that are made for the sand, would get sore here."

"No; more likely they choose the path because they would have to pay toll on the road. See those farmers working their bit of soil with wooden ploughs and teams of black buffaloes; and beyond them there is a group of Bedouins, with black tents, and flocks of black, long-eared goats and sheep."

Up, up, up they climbed, slowly, through constantly varying scenes, with sometimes wild and sometimes beautiful pictures close at hand; while far behind these were views of the plain and of Beirût and of the sea. Up and up for hours, until at last towards noon the highest part of the pass was reached.

Then they crossed to the steep eastern side, and the rapid descent began towards the great plain and the Anti-Lebanon range beyond.

"Cousin Will," said Harry, "I do n't like this kind of driving: six horses on the gallop down these hills and around these curves!"

"Neither do I like it. But the driver and horses are used to it, and I suppose there is not much danger, if only nothing breaks. How different a view this is from the one on the western side! There is no sea here, only the rich plain, seven miles wide, and stretching as far as we can see, north and south. Away to the north, farther than we can see, lies Baalbec."

At the top of a long descent the stage stopped, and the guard climbed to the ground.

"What is the trouble now?" wondered Harry.

The guard went to each side of the stage and loosened from the hooks on which they hung two skates—heavy flat pieces of iron. These he placed just in front of the rear wheels, so that when the stage started the wheels would run on them and rest there. The skates were held to their places by strong chains. The effect was the same as if he had chained the wheels, only instead of the wear coming upon the tires, it was transferred to the broad skates.

The horses were started, and with a strain and a jolt the wheels came to their place, and the steepest part of the descent began.

But the using of the skates seemed to have no effect in lessening the speed. It only relieved the pole horses somewhat and saved the guard the trouble of holding the brake, which was now left wholly and carelessly unwound.

The road zigzagged down the mountain, doubling back and forth on itself, with the almost perpendicular precipice now on one side and now on the other.

It was in one of the most dangerous of these places that the forward horse on the inside took fright and tried to run. But for a horse to do that was seemingly nothing unusual in these regions. The driver took it coolly. The guard did not even put on the brake. But they went faster and faster, and the other horses were becoming excited. Still the men were perfectly cool. Yet the road was narrow, and if a single wheel went over the edge the whole would go. They would fall at least thirty feet to a ledge that might possibly stop them. If it did not, there would be no stopping till they were all dead together at the foot of the precipice. Still they rushed along unconcernedly, and no doubt all would have gone well, and the horse soon have tired itself out or been controlled; but suddenly the rein that held the leaders broke. The three horses were wholly loose, and the most badly frightened one was pressing the others towards the edge.

That ended the unconcern of the men. The frightened driver shouted to wind the brake, and tugged with all his might on the pole horses. The guard sprang to the loosened brake, though it seemed hardly possible that it would hold against the three horses even if he could wind it in time. The swaying of the stage hindered him. It almost pitched him from his hold. But it was his and their only hope now. Just ahead was another zigzag; they could never pass it at the rate they were going. He was desperate. Would the brake hold when it was wound? Now it was wound. He strained at it with all his might; he almost lost his hold again with fear, for it would not grip! The wheels were whirling on as fast as before.

Then Will leaned forward, and seizing the brake, and bracing himself, with all his strength wrenched it a foot farther. Slower, slower; another wrench, hardly more than an inch this time; slower. It was enough; the horses felt the strain; it held them; they began plunging.

"Down, down to their heads!" the driver shouted to the guard.

He sprang in among them, for he was a brave fellow. A passenger followed him out of the window. The danger was over; but when those panting, trembling horses stopped there was no more than a foot between them all and death, over the precipice.

Harry breathed again.

Presently Will said, "I have been in many dangerous places, but, as far as I know, that was the narrowest escape with my life I ever had. If the stage had gone over there would have been no escape for us; we were in the worst place possible, on the covered top. The others might have jumped. Think how your mother will thank God, Harry; and so may we that it is no worse."

The harness was repaired, and in a few minutes they were on their way again. But after the very next change of horses they had trouble again, though of a different sort. This time it was with a kicking horse. The risk was not nearly as great as before, though, with the style of road they were on, they were by no means safe.

"The wisest thing for us to do," said Will, "is to find seats nearer the ground; at any rate until we change horses again."

The stage had come to a stand-still, with the wild horse partly in and partly out of his harness, and plunging dangerously. Several times he threw himself. Again and again he tangled himself in the traces. Once they had to cut a trace.

Some of the passengers insisted on walking ahead. But that made the matter worse, for when they were overtaken, and the stage had stopped to pick them up, the same programme had to be repeated before they could start again.

At last the driver found there was but one thing to do. He took the heavy raw-hide whip, and, as the guard let go the horses' heads and sprang back to his place, he used it over and over with all his strength on the frightened horse. The horse forgot to kick, and started with the others on the run. But they were soon controlled. Each time they started the process was repeated successfully.

At last they reached the foot of the mountain in safety. A little farther on over a straight road, and they came to the half-way station—the noon halting place—at Sthorer.

"On our way back from Damascus," said Will, "we shall leave the diligence at this station, and strike off towards the north to Baalbec. I will try and arrange now for a guide and horses to be ready for us."

The bargain was made with the station-master. He promised to furnish the horses, and go with them as guide. At one o'clock the stage was ready. They took their places again.

For seven miles across the plain the road was straight as an arrow. The horses were put to the gallop. They crossed the river Litany. They rolled on past farmers at work on their rich land, past shepherds, past travellers on foot and on horseback, with donkeys and with camels. They reached the Anti-Lebanon range.

The ascent here was much more gradual, and the scenery less grand, than on the Lebanon range. Very soon they had left all the greenness and fertility behind them. All the afternoon they rode. The roads were very dry. Their clothes were covered with the white dust. It was hot and close. They were shut in by bare white hills.

Late in the day suddenly, close before them at a turn in the valley, appeared a strip of the richest green against the white sand, trees of many sorts, vines, bushes, grass; all crowded together in one mass of greenness. They swept into it, and it seemed at once as though they were in another land, as though the legends of the East were realities, and there were in truth Aladdin's lamp, and the wonder-working genii, who had transferred them in a flash from one world to another, the change was so sudden and so complete. They had reached the valley of the Abana, and were already in the suburbs of Damascus.

"This is beautiful beyond anything I had anticipated," said Will; "trees arching the road with their branches, the sight and the sound of the rushing river, bits of green meadow wherever the trees give room for them, with the grass set thick with fiery red poppies; it is beautiful in the extreme, in contrast with what we have been riding through to reach it. And see these larger openings where the water is stiller, and where the banks and wider meadows are covered with groups of brightly dressed men and women, and grazing horses and camels, with domes and white minarets in the distance showing against the sky. It is like the old pictures we see of the 'lands of the blessed' and the 'Happy Isles,' only here none of the customary angels are just now in sight."

At six o'clock they reached the diligence station. They found their way to the one good hotel of the city. Their long day's ride was ended. They were in Damascus.

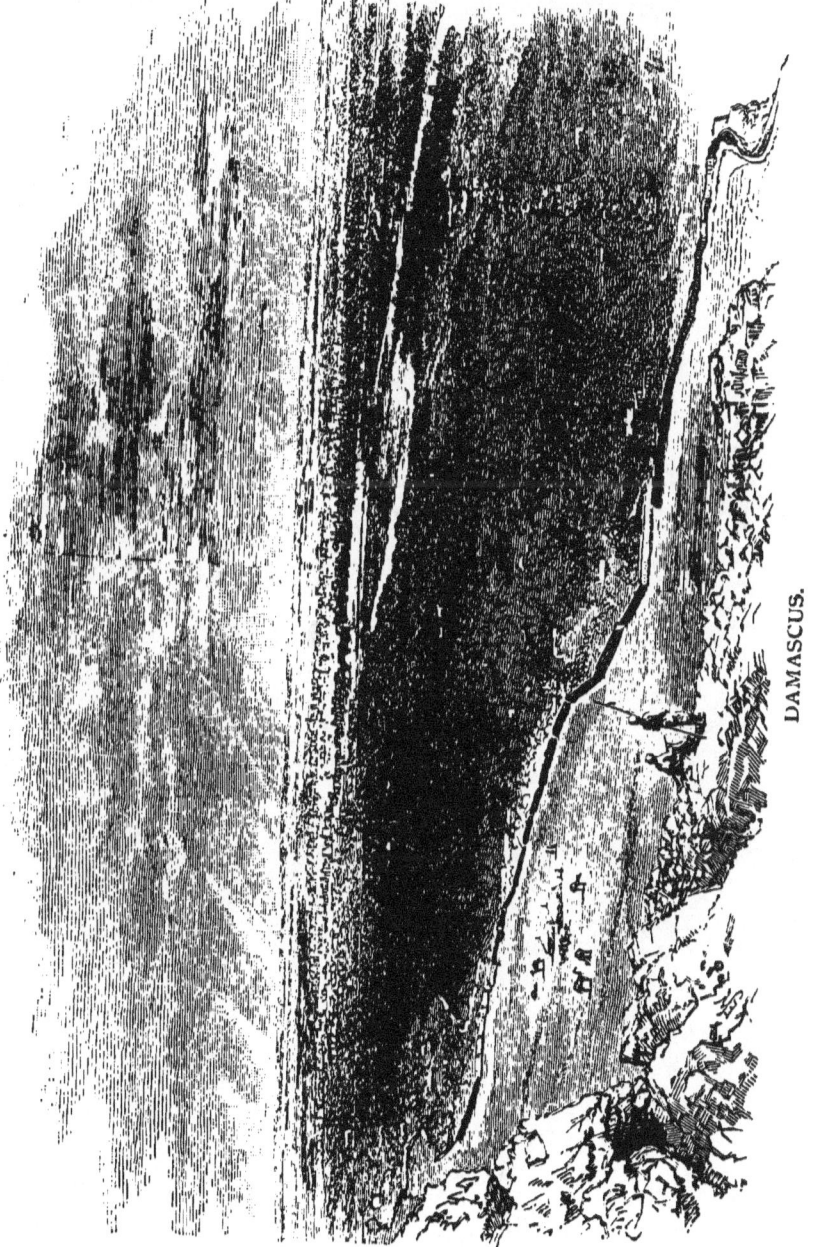
DAMASCUS.

CHAPTER XII.

DAMASCUS.

HARRY and Will are sitting under the citron-trees by the marble-inclosed fountain in the inner court of the hotel, waiting for breakfast.

"Harry, do you know how old this city of Damascus is?"

"Thousands of years old, I suppose."

"No one knows just its age, but it is one of the very oldest cities in all the world. I was kept half awake a good part of last night by the dogs, that seem to be noisier here than they are even in Constantinople. I wish I could describe the things which I half dreamed and half thought about, which tradition and history say happened here in that far past time. For one thing, I seemed to see two altars on the eastern horizon. On the one altar there was an offering of fruits, and on the other there was a lamb. There were two men near by, and soon they were struggling together, and the one killed the other, and his blood ran down and stained to a bright red all the sand. They were Cain and Abel. Cain fled away and disappeared in a cave in the mountain. It seemed like a real picture, instead of only my thought of one of the Mohammedan traditions, which accounts in that way for the red color of Mount Kasiun, lying just outside of the city walls. They say that Abel was slain there, and that his blood stains the hill. Therefore they call it Kasiun, 'Red Hill.'

"Then came another picture, of a company of travellers moving slowly over the desert, through dust and heat such as we suffered from yesterday; and coming, as we did, to the shade of trees, and to meadows and running waters. They were journeying with long trains of camels, and with flocks of goats and sheep, and with tents and baggage. And when they reached the running waters and the green fields of the Abana a procession from the city came to meet them. Then there was formal salutation in the Eastern style, the chief men embracing each other with their heads bowed on each other's shoulders, first on one shoulder and then on the other. And when they had saluted each other, they passed on and out of sight. The leader among the travellers was an old man, dark and stately, and of most reverend aspect. He was the patriarch Abraham who once lived in Damascus, and reigned here as king, according to the Mohammedans. They consider him one of their greatest prophets. They rank him next to Mohammed.

"Then I saw two armies in line of battle, placed against each other and waiting for the command to advance. It was not near Damascus; it was far away on the borders of Canaan, that the armies were opposed to each other; but one of them, and the one that seemed much the more powerful of the two, belonged to Damascus. The other was the army of the Israelites. The battle was joined, and the Israelites were victorious. Then I saw that great Damascus became tributary for a while to King David.

"After that there appeared another company approaching the city walls. Among them was Mohammed. Presently he withdrew from the others, and took his stand on the crest of the mountain where it overlooks the whole beautiful city and plain. As he stood there and saw the wonderful beauty before him, he exclaimed, 'A man can enter Paradise but once; I prefer to wait and enter the Paradise above.' Then he turned down the mountain and rode away from Damascus towards the desert."

"What mountain was that?" asked Harry.

"Mount Kasiun again. The view from it is one of the most wonderful in the world. We will get donkeys and ride there ourselves after breakfast.

"And the next thing I saw was a group of

horsemen on the road from Jerusalem. They were all Jews and with stern, dark faces. They were drawing near to the walls of the city. Suddenly a most brilliant light flashed about them, and one of the men fell to the ground. It was Saul of Tarsus, and there was wonder and confusion among them all. After a time the fallen man arose, but he could not walk by himself. He seemed to be blind. The others took him by the hand and led him towards the city. And they entered the gate and came to a long and crowded street. No one took much notice of them. They went on until they reached the house they sought. The entrance was only a narrow doorway in a high, windowless wall. They knocked. The door was opened and they disappeared within.*

"And after that the only thing I saw was a very long procession. And it was composed of all the rulers who have governed in Damascus ever since it began to be a city. They wore jewelled crowns, and carried sceptres, and dressed in brilliantly colored robes, and moved so swiftly that it was like a line of light. A good part of all the nationalities of the Old World were there, and the last of the line were Turks.

"The dogs must have lessened their howling

* Acts 9:3-25.

about that time. I went sound asleep and slept till daylight."

After breakfast Will and Harry went with donkeys and a guide to the summit of Mount Kasiun. Near the top they dismounted, and climbing a little higher, stood at the highest point, beside a small arched and domed building of stone and stucco. They could look down a thousand feet, and far, far off over green Damascus to the line of yellow desert that showed dimly beyond. At their right was a wild gorge, with the new Beirût road showing like a white thread at the bottom of it. Behind them and on both sides were bare mountains, excepting on the extreme right, where Mount Hermon towered, not bare, but covered with snow. In the foreground, between them and the city, with its domes and minarets and white houses among green trees, were clusters of round-topped stone mills and a treeless cemetery, and reaches of sand and hedges of cactus.

The city itself and its orchards lay like an island in the midst of an ocean of sand which was shoreless north, south, and east, as far as the eye could reach into the hazy, golden-tinged distance.

"And this, Harry, is the world-renowned view of Damascus! I am not disappointed in it."

"I suppose it was here," said Harry, "that Mohammed stood when he compared Damascus with Paradise."

"Yes, this vaulted monument is on the spot where tradition says he stood at the time."

They descended and reëntered the city. They roamed where they would through its narrow streets. They found the street called "Straight" by the guides for the benefit of travellers (but among themselves it is the "Street of Bazaars"). The "house of Judas" was shown them, and the "house of Ananias."

"Do you think we can trust much to these traditions of places?" asked Harry.

"Not at all to some of them. Others may be correct. I think that the best way in all our Syrian travel will be to think, 'Just here, or else in places close by with like surroundings, such and such things occurred.' To try and determine with exactness disputed localities would often take time that might be used to much better advantage in other ways. For example, we are outside now of the city, and there, by that walled-up gateway, was the place, the guide tells us, where Paul escaped when his friends lowered him at night in a basket from the top of the wall, helped (according to the guide) by Joseph the gate-keeper, who was martyred not long after for his part in the escape.* It may be the very place; but whether it is or not, certainly there, just beyond, is something that makes the event seem very real and near. Do you see that little house on the top of the wall? If there was a fugitive inside the city to-day, and his enemies were watching the gates to seize him, if only he had friends in that house it would be the easiest thing in the world, when night came, for them to lower him from the latticed window just at the edge of the wall, and send him away safe to the desert."

"I should think smuggling would have been easy in those times," said Harry.

"Yes, excepting when they had watchmen on the walls and patrols outside. But even those, it is likely, could often be evaded. You know that much the same thing happened at Jericho when the spies of Joshua were almost captured inside the walls. They could not escape by the gates; but Rahab's house, where they were in hiding, was built just as that one is, on the wall. She let them down by a rope through the window, and then told them to flee away to the mountain lest the pursuers should overtake them, and to hide there three days until their enemies had returned. Then they could safely go their way to the camp of the Israelites.†

* Acts 9 : 25 ; 2 Cor. 11 : 33.   † Josh. 2 : 15, 16.

"Now we must ride away from the walls over this wide and level road, with a few houses here and there, and trees and inclosed gardens. Not far off, the guide says, we shall come to the place where Saul was converted."

Presently they reached the place. It was a green spot at the side of the road a few square yards in area. The roadway was curved to one side, as though to avoid desecrating the holy place, and had been worn away many inches below its grassy level during the years that had passed since the time of the miracle, or of the tradition which located here the miracle of the conversion.

"To-day," said Harry, "it really seems as though we were in Bible lands."

They visited the different quarters of the city— the Jews' quarter, the Mohammedan quarter, where the house-windows are all shut in with lattice-work, and where only veiled women are seen in the streets, and the Christian quarter, where there was a terrible massacre no longer ago than 1860.

They visited the Grand Mosque, which is to Damascus what St. Sophia is to Constantinople and St. Peter's to Rome, and the bazaars, that are like long covered streets, each street given to its special trade or work.

At one place in these covered bazaars they turned through a narrow doorway, then up a rough flight of stairs that belonged to a private house, through another door, and so out to the roof of the house and bazaar. It was the only way they could reach what seemed to them the most interesting relic in Damascus—a fragment of an old ruin, the so-called "Triumphal Arch." The great cross stones were most carefully laid, and they and the capitals of the supporting columns were beautifully and richly carved. The columns themselves could not be seen.

"They must be very, very old," said Harry, "because parts are so worn, and because of the surroundings."

"There is another reason. It was built before the arch was used as commonly in architecture as it is now. The columns, you see, were so placed that the long stones of the roof could be laid flat from one to the other. The only approach to the shape of an arch is here, where these two stones are set against each other, end to end, like the sides of a triangle.

"It is no 'triumphal arch,' but may be a fragment left from some great temple; and a wonderful temple it must have been, if the whole was on a scale to compare with the part."

CHAPTER XIII.

A TURKISH BATH.

"Harry," asked Cousin Will, "how would you like to take a genuine Turkish bath to-day? There is no better place in all the East for it than Damascus."

"I'm rather afraid to try one," answered Harry.

Will laughed. "Why?"

"I'm afraid the washermen would soak me and rub me too much, as they do their own people, who are used to it."

"It isn't as hard as you think; but I will teach you words enough, so you can stop them and explain if they get to kneading you too actively."

They went to one of the finest of the many bathing establishments of the city. Entering, they found the inner room floored with marble mosaics. In the centre of it was a large fountain of running water. Around the sides, and reached by steps, were carpeted alcoves; and against the three sides of these alcoves lounges were arranged, covered with rugs and pillows.

Harry and Will were conducted to one of the alcoves. When they had disrobed behind screens of towels held by attendants, they were wrapped from head to foot in towels that were large enough for sheets. Then two muscular, scantily-clothed bathmen took charge of them, and led them from the room.

An hour later, when they met in the alcove again, Harry told Will what his experience had been.

"My big Turk proved to be a good-natured fellow. He seemed quite to enjoy steaming and sousing and scrubbing me. We went out of this room slowly through several smaller ones, and through narrow passage-ways. All of them were of stone, and each was hotter than the one before it. The man had given me a pair of wooden clogs to walk with. I thought they were to keep my feet off the wet marble, or perhaps to keep me from slipping. They were so clumsy and it was so hard walking I slipped them off, or rather, I stopped trying to keep them on, and they slipped off of themselves. But the stone floor was piping hot from a fire underneath. I was glad enough to get on to the clogs again.

"By-and-by I was set down on a stone seat by the wall and left there. The bathman went off, I did n't know where. There was no light in the stone room excepting what came through narrow slits in the ceiling. It would have made a fine dungeon. It was not solitary confinement, though; there was another criminal there, looking as forlorn as I suppose I looked, wrapped in white towels and set on a stone. But I did not feel forlorn. It was jolly.

"All this time I was as warm as toast. The air was hot, but the place was so full of moisture that it was a pleasant heat. The floors and walls were dripping wet, and there were noisy fountains all about of cold and hot water. Before long I was all in a sweat. It was what the man was waiting for. He came back and felt of me, and then took me off into a corner and set me down again, this time on the floor, close by one of the stone basins. He squatted, more gracefully than I could, cross-legged beside me. I had supposed that somewhere I would be soused into the hot water; but instead, he dipped out the water and soused it by the bucketful over and over me. Then he soaped me all over, and then he rinsed me. By that time my skin was in the right condition; so he put on a rough sort of mitten, and began scrubbing me, turning me over and over on the marble floor to make thorough work of it. When he was satisfied he poured more water over me, wrapped me in dry towels, and brought me out. Here I am. I wonder if they are through with me?"

"Yes," said Will, "you have nothing to do now but to lie back among the pillows and enjoy as long as you choose the after-pleasantness of a Turkish bath. Dream a while. It will be easy to do it whether you go sound asleep or not. Then you can dress, drink if you like the little cup of black coffee they will bring you, and go your way with me out into the heat and noise of the streets again."

"Cousin Will, I think a Turkish bath is one of the very nicest things in the world."

"So it is, when it is taken in Damascus."

CHAPTER XIV.

DAMASCUS TO BAALBEC.

"To-day," said Will, "we must leave all this great beauty, this rushing water and these fountains and gardens and covered streets crowded with life and color. It is a pleasant picture to have for our very own all our lives long. I think we must send Nellie a bit of it. You remember how bright and musical the water was the day we went up Mount Kasiun. We will send her this:

THE WATER-FALL.

Your tones are silvery sweet
Where foam and wavelet meet
With ceaseless beat.

You touch the rocky keys;
Far through the aisles of trees
The music flees;

It ever flows as low
As softest breezes go
With cadence slow;

As softly ebbs and swells
As though in distant dells
Rang chimes of bells.

God's temple of the hills
Is here. Fit music fills
It from your rills.

But there are more pictures elsewhere for us to find, some delicate and some rugged. The next one is at Baalbec. If we can get seats in the night post to Sthorer, we can breakfast there and reach Baalbec to-morrow noon."

But when they came to the office they found that all the seats by the night stage had been taken. They engaged places instead for the next morning. And when the next morning came they said good-by to Damascus. By noon they had safely retraced their route over the Anti-Lebanon range to Sthorer. There they found Andrea, the station-keeper, ready with saddled horses to guide them to Baalbec.

Will and Harry were quietly eating their dinner before starting, when a man, a stranger, appeared at the door of the room. The minute Andrea saw him he sprang up and rushed at him, and seizing him by the throat tried to force him away from the house. The two were separated; but after a minute the hubbub began again. A crowd gathered, shouting and excited. An Arab darted off, and came running back with his gun. Andrea got his gun. It looked very much as though there was to be a general fight. Will and Harry recognized the fact then that they were in lawless regions. They expected every instant to hear shots; and if the firing once began among such a crowd of wild-looking fellows there was no knowing how or when it would end. But gradually the confusion subsided. Andrea came back, sullen and fierce. The crowd dispersed.

They thought they had engaged rather a rough specimen for their guide. He tried to tell them, in the little English he knew, what the trouble was all about. It proved to be about themselves. The man who had come to the door wanted to bargain with them to be their guide to Baalbec. Andrea did not want the bargain already made with himself to be interfered with, and he took the means he deemed best to prevent it.

After dinner they mounted and rode away towards the north, up the valley, with the Lebanon range, grand and beautiful, on the left, and the lower Anti-Lebanon range on the right. Most of their way at first was through villages and over cultivated ground and pasture-land.

When they had made half the distance they passed a large khan for the accommodation of travellers and shepherds. Many flocks of sheep and goats were grazing near by, and camels and horses. Men were sitting about, most of them heavily armed, sipping from their little cups of black coffee, and resting in the shade. Beyond that the way was wilder and lonelier. All the afternoon they rode.

"Do n't you think we ought to see the ruins from that ridge ahead?" asked Harry.

"Yes," answered Will; "it is getting late, and the guide says we can see them for an hour before we reach the village."

But it was only after they had passed that ridge and several besides that at last they saw, far ahead, the trees and houses and ruins of Baalbec. They stopped their horses and stood for a while, looking and thinking, while the sun sank low towards the tops of Lebanon.

Presently Harry spoke. "Cousin Will, I am disappointed."

"So am I to some extent. The ruins are not nearly as imposing from this distance as I supposed they would be. But we are a long way off. Wait until we are among them. I imagine it will be very different then."

They rode rapidly forward again. On their left were the remains of a small ruined temple—only a few stone columns that had been taken from the greatly older and vaster ruins beyond. They were left standing now, in a small circle, with heavy cross-stones for the roof, some of them still in place and some fallen to the ground.

"It is nothing," said Andrea, as Harry questioned him; "nothing at all but only one little speck compared with what you shall see."

Bright little Syrian children from the village, who were playing there, watched the travellers curiously as they turned from the path and rode around the ruin. Farther on there were more children. They formed in line at the side of the path, and as Will and Harry passed saluted them with cries of "Good morning, good morning!" hoping for gifts of backsheesh in return, and ignorant of the difference in English between "good morning" and "good evening."

Just before entering the town the guide asked if they wished to stop there and visit the quarries from which most of the stone for the temples had been taken.

"Is it far away?" asked Will.

"No; only a minute."

"Then we will go now."

And to Harry Will said, "We shall find in this quarry something that has always greatly interested me—one of the largest hewn stones in the world. It is cut and squared and finished to a line, nearly ready to be taken away and placed in the temple wall. It measures sixty-nine feet in length, seventeen in height, and fourteen in width."

They found the quarry only a few rods distant from the main path, over the slope of a rough hill; and there in the middle of it, with lesser giants all about, lay the one great giant of which they had been speaking. They rode to the side of it, and it towered high above them as they sat on their horses. They walked around it. Harry dismounted and clambered to its top.

"It seems as though I was on top of a flat-roofed house," he shouted down, "if only the stone was hollowed out and windows and doors cut in it."

"Men who were able to shape it and move it might have done that if they had liked," answered Will.

"Who were those men?"

"Come down from your perch and I will tell you about them."

Harry clambered down, and they rode on towards the town.

"No one knows certainly who the first builders were of the temples of Baalbec," said Will. "Some think that Baalbec is the same as the Bible 'Baal-gad,'* and that these stones were cut and laid by king Solomon. We know, from the foundations of the temple area at Jerusalem, that the Jews understood such work. All the Mohammedan traditions point to some 'Suleiman,' and apparently to him as the builder. The oldest parts of the ruins are certainly as old as those

* Josh. 11:17; 13:5.

times, and they may be much older.* But all periods are represented in Baalbec. The ruins of the oldest temples were used for newer ones, and the ruins of those in turn for newer still, over and over, down almost to present times. Very likely parts of the Temple of the Sun or of Jupiter are in the rough walls of the little native houses that we have been passing; and pieces of the slenderer columns are just the thing for rollers, such as we have noticed on the roofs, for smoothing and hardening their clay covering."

"Did all the stone for the temples come first from those quarries?" asked Harry.

"Most of it. The foundations and the walls and the greater part of the columns are of the same dull-white limestone. But many of the columns were of the hardest kind of granite, most beautifully polished and carved. There are fragments of them now all about the ruins. Those must have been brought from Egypt. There is nothing of the sort nearer. I once compared two bits of stone, one from the Temple of the Sphinx in Egypt, and the other from these ruins. They were exactly alike."

"It must have been hard work bringing the columns so far," said Harry.

* But probably the weight of authority would make Baalbec a different place from "Baal-gad," and located farther south.

"Yes. We do not know how it was done."

"I don't wonder that they got discouraged with that great fellow in the quarry, and had to leave it there."

"Oh, no; that was not the reason for leaving it. They were able to move it if they had cared to. We shall find other single stones just about as large in one of the foundation walls."

After five hours of riding from Sthorer they passed through a high gateway into a neat whitewashed inclosure and to the door of the khan where they were to lodge. They were glad to dismount. It had been a hard ride.

CHAPTER XV.

RETURN TO BEIRÛT.

"I want my first near view of these famous ruins of Baalbec to be by starlight," said Will. "It is too late any way to explore them thoroughly before to-morrow; so we will rest a while and have dinner, and then go out and find them in the dark."

Two hours later, when it was wholly dark, excepting for the brilliant starlight, Will and Harry were in the midst of the ruins. They were standing alone below the six lonely columns of the "Great Temple." Looking far up towards the sky they could see there the overhanging entablature and the outline of the rich Corinthian capitals, dark against the stars, with the graceful columns underneath.

Said Will, "We were disappointed in the first view. This is all that I looked for, and more. Nothing of the kind could well be more impressive."

"It was a heathen temple once," said Harry; "but it seems now as though it was a temple of God."

"Yes," answered Will; "in its ruin it is God's temple; and it seems to me to-night as though God was in his temple."

The whole of the next morning was spent in the town and among the ruins.

"I had no idea there was so much of a village here," said Harry. "In fact, I thought there was not much but ruins."

"Andrea says there are 3,500 inhabitants, but there cannot be nearly as many as that. Yet once Baalbec was as busy and prosperous as Damascus is now."

They found remains of churches and temples in different parts of the town, but the most interesting ones were grouped together around the place they had visited the evening before; and of those the most imposing were the Temple of Jupiter and the Temple of the Sun.

The view they had by daylight did not lessen the impression of the night. They explored a series of massive subterranean Roman vaults, and an Arabic temple lighted, like the Pantheon at Rome, through an opening in the centre of the dome. All about were huge, fallen columns— many of which had been thrown down by the Arabs simply for the sake of the metal that was used in fastening the parts together—and Corinthian capitals, and pieces of highly ornamented entablature and roofing. And there they found again, no more imposing in the daylight, but more beautiful, the six wonderful columns of the once wonderful "Great Temple." The pedestals of these columns, in single pieces, were about even with Will's head as he stood beside them. The circumference of the shafts is 22 feet. Each shaft, in but three pieces, is 62 feet in length, and the whole height of each, with capital and entablature, is 76 feet. There are but six columns standing now. Once there were 54, supporting the roof of a temple 290 feet long and 160 feet wide.

A few rods away is another temple, smaller than the first, but in much better preservation, and showing more rich Corinthian decoration.

And then the foundation for these immense superstructures, a vast platform 50 feet high! All of the stones in them are huge; some are like the giant they had seen in the quarry. They found the place where three of the largest are set end to end in the face of the wall.

"Why, Cousin Will," said Harry, "I thought you said these stones were a little smaller than the one in the quarry."

"So I did," answered Will. "These are about 13 feet wide and high and 63 feet long."

"Why, we have certainly walked much more than 63 feet from where this one commenced."

"But you have passed the end of the first stone. You are opposite the second one now."

"Am I? And yet I thought I was looking carefully all the time to see where they came together."

"We will go back and find the place; for one of the strange things here is, not merely how they could quarry such stones, but how, when they had them quarried and shaped, they could place them so exactly in position."

"Here is the place where they meet. No wonder I overlooked it."

"No wonder at all. Just think: after all these centuries, and after at least one great earthquake, there is no room between them even to slip in the blade of my knife!"

At two o'clock they mounted for their return to Sthorer. The people of the khan were gathered about to receive their backsheesh and to see them off. They rode out through the arched gateway, and, turning to the south, retraced the route of the previous day. Sometimes they walked their horses; sometimes they rode at a gallop. Once, when they drew rein, Will asked,

"Harry, why were you riding back there with

your teeth clenched as though you were charging a battery?"

"Was I? I didn't know it. But going over loose stones like these on the run isn't much like our home riding."

"The horses are trained to it. But if we do any more horseback-riding in Syria we will have the native saddle, with high pummel and cantel and with covered wooden stirrups. I meant to have had them this time. They are more like what our Western riders at home use, and I like them better for rough work than these low English saddles and iron stirrups."

At seven they were back safely at Sthorer. There they were glad to find two young Americans travelling with horses to Beirût. The greetings on both sides were cordial and the talk earnest for the little time they had together. The strangers were planning to leave the East by the next steamer from Beirût.

"Are the horses you have good ones?" asked Will.

"Yes, first rate; the best we could find in Jerusalem."

"And they and your man belong in Jerusalem and will have to go back there?"

"Yes."

"I believe that here is just the chance that

Harry and I want. If we can make a bargain with your man, we will take him and his horses and go by land to Jerusalem instead of by steamer to Jaffa. We will travel without tents, stopping nights where we can along the way—at the hospices, with the Arabs, wherever we happen to be."

"You could not do better. There is no other way you could be as independent and gain as good an idea of the country and the people. Where shall you be to-morrow in Beirût?"

"At the Hotel Oriental."

"We will find you there."

Will and Harry were to start at midnight. They went to their rooms for a short sleep before the arrival of the post. The others would follow on horseback early in the morning.

The next day in Beirût the proposed arrangement was carried out. By night Will and Harry were ready, with four horses engaged and two men, for the journey to Jerusalem. Their route was to be south along the coast as far as Mount Carmel, then inland to the Sea of Galilee, and then south again, across the plain of Esdraelon, through Samaria, to Jerusalem.

A written agreement had been made with the men, defining each day's route and arranging for the details of the journey. They were to start the next day.

Said Will, as he and Harry sat that evening in their room,

"It seems to me that that meeting with Davis and Norris at Sthorer was an exceedingly providential thing. Excepting for it we would have been on our way now by to-day's steamer to Jaffa; but, instead, we have arranged exactly the plan which I would have chosen in preference to any other."

CHAPTER XVI.

BEIRÛT TO THE DAMUR.

THERE is a knock at the door.

"Come in."

Elias, entering respectfully, "It is six o'clock, sir."

"Are the horses ready?"

"Yes, sir, they are at the door with Hassan."

"Come, Harry. Our men are prompt."

The party that filed through the streets of Beirût on that pleasant May morning was by no means as large as "a caravan to Mecca." Besides William and Harry there was "Abraham Elias," engaged as "servant, guide, and interpreter." He was a Syrian from the Lebanon, but had picked up a few English words and manners in serving at the hotels and as guide. He wore "Frank clothes," excepting the head-dress. That was native, a large silk handkerchief of bright colors, falling back over the neck and shoulders to protect them from the sun, and held in place by a knotted cord around the forehead. He carried a large horse pistol, was dark, with a fiercely curled moustache, black eyes, and black hair.

But in spite of his fine looks, it took only a short time to prove him either stupid or rascally, it was hard telling which. Most likely there was a combination of both qualities. He knew much less of English than an interpreter ought to know, was very careless; but was a fair guide, and apparently honest in money matters, which latter fact he appeared to pride himself in as something unusual.

"Hassan" was the "muktari," in charge of the horses and baggage. He was wholly native, picturesque, tough, good-natured, a Mohammedan. His dress a white turban wound about a crimson "fez," a loose blue jacket, red vest, sash, white baggy trousers to the knee, bare shins, red pointed, turned-up shoes. He was armed with a long gun, and generally rode perched on top of the load carried by the stout baggage horse. The baggage consisted only of two small boxes, shawls and blankets, and a reserve supply of needed provisions. Will was mounted on a stout gray horse. Harry rode a smaller bay. In leaving the city the "caravan" took the road leading south towards Sidon, nine hours distant—about twenty-seven miles. At first the way was over great hills of drifted sand, like drifted snow. Yet the sand-hills lay a full mile back from the sea. It was like a small desert.

"Where does it all come from?" asked Harry. "It seems out of place here, so near the city and the mountains, and with everything fertile and green and beautiful close up to it."

"It came last from the sea," answered Will, "drifted inland by the strong southerly winds; but where the sea found it is uncertain. Some think the currents brought it all the way from the African shore; others, that it came from the mouth of the Nile; others, from the wash of the rivers along the Syrian coast. It is certainly a far traveller; and as certainly it is an unwelcome one. Wherever it came from, it is doing immense damage here. It has changed all this region from rich fields into a desert."

Soon they were on the seashore, riding close by the waves that broke musically over the pebbles, or in other places more roughly and with deeper music against ledges of seaweed-covered rocks. During most of the day the course was the same, close by the waves on the sandy beach, but sometimes above the water over rough, stony, cliffs and bold headlands.

They were about an hour south of Beirût when Harry remarked,

"What lots of travellers there are here—men and women and children, with donkeys and horses and camels, rich and poor, crowds of them!"

"It must be unusual," said Will. "Elias, where are all these people flocking?"

"To see a prophet, sir. Most of them to get cured, sir."

"Where is the prophet?"

"He has a hut on the shore, sir, about an hour from here. We shall pass it."

"Who is he? What does he say about himself?"

"He had been sick many years. Then he had a vision. It was about a month ago. An angel came and told him if he would go to the sea and bathe and eat certain kinds of food, in a month he would be well. The time now is more than half gone, sir, and the prophet is almost cured, and he has himself cured many people just by touching them. So now all who can are flocking to see him. Some of them come a very long way, sir."

"It would be a blessed thing for this people," said Will to Harry, "if they were as ready to believe in the true revelation from God as they are in these false revelations. It makes me think of the Saviour's prediction, that many false prophets would arise after him, who would deceive many."*

Riding on, they soon reached the hut of the

* Matt. 24:11.

prophet, with crowds gathered about it over the sand in a sheltered part of the shore. They stopped their horses to watch the picturesque groups. But they did not dismount. In a few minutes they rode on again towards the river Damur and their noon camping-ground.

"Cousin Will, there is another of those khans. We have seen so many of them without stopping, suppose we stop at this and find what they are like inside."

"Yes. We will stop and rest a while here."

They dismounted and gave their horses to Elias. The khan was a low, one-story structure built of rough stone, with a porch on the shady side raised a few inches from the ground. Within were two or three dark, dismal rooms.

"I wouldn't want to sleep in there," said Harry. "It's dreadfully dark and dirty, and besides I dare say it swarms with fleas."

"There is no doubt of that," said Will. "But you may have to sleep in worse places before the trip is over. It is hardly likely though."

The owner of the khan spread straw mats on the floor of the shady porch. They lay down and rested, with their shawls for pillows, while the man went away to prepare their cups of coffee over a brazier full of coals in one of the dark rooms.

Soon the coffee was brought, black and thick, in tiny china cups holding about two table-spoonfuls each. They sipped it slowly, while Elias near by puffed contentedly at a nargileh.

"Bring the horses, Elias."

"Yes, sir."

They mounted, and rode again towards the Damur. As they crossed a very rocky strip of shore, where the reefs reached out into the sea, making foam and currents and eddies, they saw a man wading in the water. He was carrying something in his hand, Harry could not make out what.

"See how carefully he moves, as though he was afraid of slipping, or, more likely, of frightening something. Maybe he is crabbing," said Harry.

Suddenly the man swung his arm and threw off over the water what he had been holding. He threw it with a whirling motion that made it spread gracefully before it fell, and showed it to be a large circular net. He was a fisherman. Again and again he threw the net, but seemingly with poor success, until they were out of sight.

"This was always a noted coast for fisheries," said Will. "No doubt, away back in Old Testament times, men were fishing here in this same way, with the same kind of nets. One of the most noted of the old prophecies concerning Tyre tells of the time to come when fishermen would spread their nets to dry on rocks that were covered then with the buildings of the prosperous city."*

"I'm getting hungry," said Harry. "It must be nearly noon."

"Yes; and there ahead is the new bridge over the Damur. We will lunch there. It is the only place anywhere about, excepting another miserable khan just beyond, that will give us the needed shade."

"There is hardly a tree in sight, is there?" said Harry. "The whole country seems bare of them."

"But how beautiful and how large and thick the clumps of oleanders are! If the sun was only a little lower they would give shadow enough for us. See what a pink crowd of them there is about that tumble-down ruin on the river just below the new bridge."

"Do you know," said Harry, "what they make me think of by the way they grow? Of neglected lilac-bushes at home, in the yards of old country houses; only here they grow wild anywhere along the road. What is that ruin?"

"It is the remains of the old bridge, or, rather,

* Ezek. 26:14.

of the old bridges; for again and again new ones have been built on the old Roman foundations, only to be mastered in time by the quiet little river flowing here softly now at our feet as though it never had the slightest thought of doing anybody or anything one bit of harm. But the quiet little river is a roaring giant sometimes. It drains a great stretch of mountainous country, so that heavy rains and melting snows affect it very quickly. But the new bridge that we reach now is likely to last. Here is a good place, in the shadow of this buttress, to dismount and lunch; only we are likely enough to be interrupted by passers-by. There comes a line of camels now, with their drivers; but no matter; we do not object to that; and if the people will stop and talk to us, and let us know what they are thinking about and what their ways of life are, so much the better. Get the lunch from the saddle-bags, Elias; and if you want coffee you can boil it at the little fire of sticks which those men have yonder by that flock of black goats."

"Oh, but this tastes good!" exclaimed Harry as they ate; "chickens and bread and honey and eggs and egg-shaped Jaffa oranges and figs. I wonder what they will give us in the places where we stop nights? Sometimes good food and sometimes bad, I imagine."

Two native women came walking down towards the bridge. One was old and blear-eyed; the other was younger and more attractive. They sat down on the ground near the servants and began an earnest conversation with them. The faces of both were deeply tattooed in stars and lines and squares.

"I never saw anything like that before," said Harry; "and I suppose they think it makes them handsome. I have seen sailors with tattooed hands and arms; but this is over their faces. Is it common here, do you think, tattooing like that?"

"Yes; almost all the women show more or less of it. It is the fashion. They do it by pricking the figure they want into the skin with single needles, or with bundles of them, and then binding gunpowder over the wounds. That gives the tattooing its bluish tinge. Elias, what are those women so earnest about?"

"They are talking of the prophet, sir. The old woman has been to him to get cured of her sore eyes, sir."

"Did he help her?"

"Oh, yes, sir. Her eyes are much better; at least, so she says."

CHAPTER XVII.

THE DAMUR TO SIDON.

It was pleasant resting there by the river, but our travellers had rested long enough. It was time to ride on towards Sidon.

The grazing horses were caught and saddled; the baggage was repacked. They mounted and rode again, over the sometimes sandy and sometimes stony path, southward, along the cliffs and along the shore.

"I wonder if the road is like this all the way to Sidon?" said Harry.

"Most of the way. Harry, how much do you know about Jonah?"

"About Jonah! Nothing but what the Bible tells. Does anybody?"

"He is one of the favorite prophets of the Mohammedans, and they claim that it was on this shore that he was landed by the great fish, and that he was buried here. They have built a tomb at the place; we shall pass it soon. The Koran refers to him a number of times. In one place it gives the Mohammedan version of his story. It says that the ship in which he was sailing stood still, that at last he sprang into the sea, where a great fish swallowed him, and then swam with its head above water, so as to give him air, until it cast him out on the shore.*

"The tenth chapter of the Koran is named for Jonah; and it gives also a prayer of his, offered, the Mohammedans say, from the belly of the fish. It is brief, but they consider it a very holy prayer, and often offer it in their devotions.†

"It is curious, too, what a resemblance there is between our Bible account of Jonah and some of the old Greek traditions. For example, one of them says that at Tyre (where we plan spending to-morrow night) Neptune, god of the sea, once

* "Jonas was also one of those who were sent by us [i. e., God], when he fled into the loaded ship, and those who were on board cast lots among themselves, and he was condemned, and the fish swallowed him, for he was worthy of reprehension. And if he had not been one of those who praised God, verily he would have remained in the belly thereof until the day of resurrection. And we cast him on the naked shore and he was sick, and we caused a plant of a gourd to grow up over him, and we sent him to a hundred thousand persons, or they were a greater number, and they believed, wherefore we granted them to enjoy this life for a season." Koran, chap. 37.

† "And remember Dhu' Inun (i. e., 'the dweller in the fish') when he departed in wrath and thought that we could not exercise our power over him. And he cried out in the darkness, saying, 'There is no God besides thee. Praise be unto thee! Verily, I have been one of the unjust.' Wherefore we heard him and delivered him from affliction, for so do we deliver the true believers." Koran, chap. 21.

sent out a great sea monster, which did terrible harm along the coast at every return of the tide. There was no way to appease the creature but by giving up to him Helen, the beautiful daughter of the king of the land. So Helen was chained to a rock within reach of the terrible, fire-breathing dragon. It saw her and rushed at her, and was just ready to seize her when Hercules interfered. With his drawn sword he leaped into its throat, and for three days and three nights fought there, until at last he conquered and killed the monster, and came forth, himself unharmed, excepting that his hair was singed by the heat of the place. So one of the surnames of Hercules became 'Triesperos' ('three nights').

"And on this same coast, only farther south, at Jaffa, which is the port from which Jonah sailed, the scene was laid of another and one of the most familiar of the old Greek stories, the story of Andromeda. Andromeda, like Helen, was offered to appease the fury of a sea monster. In the time of Jerome (in the fourth century) the very rock where she was said to have been chained, near the entrance of the harbor, was shown to travellers. This time it was Perseus who came to the rescue. By means of the snaky Medusa's head which he bore he was able to turn the monster to stone. So he saved the maiden.

"Then there are other Babylonian traditions. It is curious how they all seem to point with varying degrees of correctness to an event like that of which the Bible tells."

They found the "Tomb of Jonah" on a long and wide reach of sand between two promontories. It was only a low-domed structure, with a few rooms attached for the accommodation of the keeper and the many pilgrims who visit the so-called sacred place. Close by it was an ordinary khan.

On again they rode, over sand and over rocks, above and beside the sounding sea, until late in the afternoon, when they approached Sidon. On their left was the long reach of Sidon's groves and orchards; on the right the Mediterranean. Before them the shore swept in and then out with an even curve that held at its farther point, a mile away, the poor successor of the ancient mighty city of the Zidonians.

"It would seem in keeping now," said Will, "if we could meet some broken-down, old, old man, born thousands of years ago, to tell us about Sidon."

"What would he say?"

"Perhaps something like this:

"'I am the "Spirit of Sidon." I was born a most vigorous child back in the times of the patriarchs,* and I can never die until Sidon wholly ceases to be. In the time of Joshua I was advanced enough to be called 'great;'† and almost ever since, until within only a few years (only some four or five hundred years), mine has been one of the strongest and most beautiful and prosperous of all the cities of Syria, though now, alas! it is weak and ragged and forlorn every way.'

"And then, if we encouraged him to talk on, no doubt he would tell us all about the wars he has been in, especially the terrible war with the Persians in the fourth century B. C., when, although he had a large army and many allies, and thought himself very strong, he was wholly and quickly defeated, but only through the treachery of some whom he thought friends. 'It was an awful time,' he would tell us, 'and it took us a long while to recover from it. Only think of it,' he would say, 'one hundred of our chief citizens were betrayed to the Persian king;‡ and then five hundred more, who went out to try and make terms, were seized by him. They were all slain. And when my people found it was of no use to fight any longer, what do you suppose they did rather than fall into the hands of the cruel

* Gen. 10:15, 19.   † Josh. 11:8.
‡ Artaxerxes III., Ochus., B. C. 359–338.

Persians? They shut themselves up in their homes with their families, and then set fire to the houses and burned themselves to death, forty thousand of them!

"'That was 351 years before the time of Christ. Indeed, it took us a long while to recover from such an almost fatal blow as that. And then the victorious Alexander the Great came, and we were glad to open the city gates before him and receive him as our master in place of the Persians. We even helped him with our fleet in his long siege of our neighbor, Tyre. We were prosperous under the Macedonians and under the Romans; but in the time of the Crusaders, ah, then we were all broken down again; and we have never been quite ourselves since. Truly it makes me very, very sad when I see in what a condition we are now, and remember what we once were. And it is not alone that we were once so strong for battle, but we were great merchants also. We were rivals of Tyre. Our ships and our merchandise went everywhere. Why, my friend Homer, in that poem of his which you may have seen, speaks of us often and most flatteringly. Some of the bravest of the Grecian heroes of whom he tells, Achilles and Agamemnon, wore armor made by us; and they surely had need of the best. In another place he names prizes that Achilles gave to the soldiers at the funeral games held after the death of his friend Patroclus. To the swiftest runner was given a large and beautiful silver bowl, made by us.*

"'And in another place he says that the most beautiful present which Menelaus, the brother of king Agamemnon, could find for the son of his old comrade, Ulysses, was a gold and silver bowl made by our skilful workmen.† But it was not

* "And then the son of Peleus placed in sight
Prizes of swiftness: a wrought silver cup
That held six measures, and in beauty far
Excelled all others known; the cunning hands
Of the Sidonian artisans had given
Its graceful shape, and over the dark sea
Men of Phœnicia brought it, with their wares,
To the Greek harbors."
    Iliad, Bryant's Tr., B. XXIII. 911 ff.

† "Of all that in my house
Are treasured up, the choicest I will give,
And the most precious. I will give a cup
Wrought all of silver save its brim of gold.
It is the work of Vulcan. Phædimus
The hero, king of Sidon, gave it me,
When I was coming home, and underneath
His roof was sheltered. Now it shall be thine."
    Odyssey, Bryant's Tr., B. IV. 779 ff.

"I give thee here
Of all the treasures which my house contains
The fairest and most precious. I present
A goblet all of silver, save the lips,
And they are bound with gold. It is the work
Of Vulcan. Phædimus the hero, king
Of the Sidonians, gave it me when once

our work in the metals alone that he honored in his poem. He says that when the mother of the Trojan Hector wished to make an offering to the great goddess Athene, she chose rich, embroidered robes, which were woven and embroidered by our fair women.*

"'But now, alas and alas, all our glory is departed. We have no power; we manufacture almost nothing. Instead of great fleets we own only a few little fishing boats, in a harbor so choked with rocks and sand that none of your great ships could enter it if they would. Instead of the thousands of prosperous people who once dwelt here, now, alas, there are no more than one or two thousand. Indeed, we are in a most miserable condition.'

>His palace sheltered me. He gave it me
>At parting, and I now would have it thine."
>
>   Odyssey, B. XV. 143 ff.

> * "The queen
> Descended to her chamber, where the air
> Was sweet with perfumes, and in which were laid
> Her rich embroidered robes, the handiwork
> Of Sidon's damsels, whom her son had brought—
> The godlike Alexander—from the coast
> Of Sidon, when across the mighty deep
> He sailed and brought the high-born Helen thence.
> One robe most beautiful of all she chose
> To bring to Pallas, ampler than the rest,
> And many-hued; it glistened like a star,
> And lay beneath them all."
>
>   Iliad, Bryant's Tr., B. VI. 375 ff.

"And then we would try and comfort the old man by reminding him how much better off his city is than many another of the Syrian towns— than his old rival Tyre, for example; and how much good is being accomplished here, and in all the region about, by the noble band of missionary workers. And that would make us think to ask him if he did not once receive visits from the Founder of this beautiful religion which the missionaries teach.

"'Yes,' he would say, 'the Jesus Christ of whom they tell once passed here on a journey along our coasts,* and we wished that he could have remained long enough to do in this region the mighty works which he did in Capernaum and Bethsaida. If he had, I verily believe we would have repented long ago in sackcloth and ashes. As it was, we received some of his disciples who fled here and formed a church, after the stoning to death at Jerusalem of that good man Stephen.†

"'And some years after, we had a most notable visit, though we thought much less of it then than I do now, from the very man who had stood by and held the clothes of those who stoned Stephen, but who had since then been converted near Damascus (you travellers may have seen the very

* Matt. 15: 21 ff; Mark 7: 24 ff.   † Acts 11 : 19.

place), and had become a wonderfully able and successful apostle of the Lord Jesus Christ. His name was Paul. He was on his way to Rome. The ship touched here. He landed and was received by our Christians with much reverence and love.* He encouraged them greatly. He was a wonderful man. It seems to me as though it was all only yesterday, instead of more than eighteen hundred years ago.'

"Now we must suppose the talkative old man to be dismissed. The long story has brought us to the entrance of the town, and we will have to use all care not to slip on the smooth pavements, or drive over the children and the men and women in the narrow streets."

"Where are we to lodge to-night?" asked Harry.

"You have heard of the hospices of the Alps, the Hospice of St. Bernard, for example, where any who need shelter and food are received and cared for, and sent on their way without charge. The poorest pay nothing. The wealthier are expected to give according to their means. There are a number of such institutions through Palestine, most of them under the care of the Roman-catholics. We shall make use of several of them before we finish our journey. One of them, Elias

Acts 27 : 3.

says, is located here in Sidon, and he is trying to guide us to it now. I doubt, though, if he knows where it is. I haven't much faith any way in the man's fitness for the work he has engaged to do."

At last they reached the hospice. It was a large rambling old building of stone, used also as a monastery. But it was one of the church's fast days, and, according to Elias, the monks had no food for the travellers; and as nearly as they could understand him, there was no sleeping-place for them either; but they could make little sense of what he said. What could they do?

"Elias, do you know the way to the American Consul's?"

"Yes, sir."

"Then take us there."

But he did not know the way; and when after considerable wandering he succeeded in finding the place, the consul was absent.

It was coming to be rather a serious matter. They were thoroughly tired, and it was growing dark. If possible, they must find some one who could understand and speak English, and could direct them to some sort of lodging-place or tell them clearly in regard to the hospice. How about the American missionaries, whom they wished to meet but would have preferred to see after, rather than before they were lodged? Could they be found? Mr. Eddy, they were told, was away visiting some of the mountain stations; but his sister was at home.

"Find their house," said Will.

And so they wandered about again. As they walked on, hungry and tired, half angry with Elias, and somewhat so with all Sidon, a long procession filled the narrow street in front of them.

"There," Elias said, "is Miss Eddy and her school."

Will stepped forward, and upon introducing himself and Harry, was cordially welcomed. Her brother was at home, the lady said, and would be glad to meet them. His house was close by. She directed them to it.

Soon Will and Harry stood at the door. They knocked. The native servant answered.

"Is Mr. Eddy at home?"

"No, sir. He went out a few minutes ago and will not return until late."

Disappointed again! There appeared to be no help for it. They decided to go back to the hospice. They would be allowed, no doubt, to camp somewhere inside its walls, and they could look for something to eat in the shops.

But just as they were turning from the door,

two young men came out. They were Americans, Mr. Dennis, a missionary of Beirût, and his brother, from New York. The parties had never met before, but they had mutual friends, their distant homes were near each other, and besides they were Christians meeting in a far-away, unchristian land. They met almost like old acquaintances.

The brothers were two of a party of tent-travellers returning to Beirût. They were encamped, they said, just outside of the town. Mr. Eddy was there and would take tea with them, and they gave Will and Harry a cordial invitation to join the party, an invitation which they very willingly accepted.

A pleasant evening was spent, partly at the tent and partly in a visit to the prosperous girls' school under the care of the ladies of the mission. What remained of the evening and the night, all five of the travellers spent with Mr. Eddy. One and another of the native Christians came in to meet the Christians from other lands. There was conversation concerning the success and present prosperity of the mission, concerning the work and the earnest workers, and the good promise which the past and the present give for the future.

When it was time for the little company to

separate, and time, too, for the evening prayers, they asked Will to lead them in their worship. Then they separated, some to their homes, and the travellers to their welcome rest. The quiet of the night was broken only by the beating of the Mediterranean waves in the moonlight close outside their chamber windows. Whenever they half awoke the waves seemed whispering them to sleep again with soft slumber songs.

CHAPTER XVIII.

SIDON TO TYRE.

"YOUR ride to-day to Tyre will not be very different from yesterday's," said Mr. Eddy, as Will and Harry were mounting for their day's journey. "There is but little of special interest along the way. You will pass the site of old Sarepta,* but you will scarcely be able to tell when. You might stop, though, and visit some old tombs not far from here, and only a short distance off your direct road; but it is rather hard to find them. I wish I could go and show you the way."

"Elias, do you know where they are?" asked Will.

"Yes, sir."

"Are you certain? Have you been to them?"

"I think I could find them."

"I will tell you," said Mr. Eddy; "I will send my boy with you. That will be the surest way."

Cordial good-bys were spoken, and they rode away to the south. A mile or so from the town

* Luke 4:26; 1 Kings 17:9 ff.

they found the tombs they were in search of. There were great holes in the ground where excavations had been made. Clambering down into these they reached the entrances to the stone chambers, which had once been carefully-kept and sacred resting-places of the dead. Now they were half filled with dirt. The stucco-work was defaced and broken. The narrow recesses in the sides, where the embalmed bodies once rested in richly-carved sarcophagi, were open and empty. In one place only there remained a nearly perfect sarcophagus; but it had long before been opened and rifled.

This detour had led them away from the seashore. They rode now through a rich farming region, with wide fields of ripened grain on either side. In some places the harvesters were already at work, with modern Ruths gleaning after them beside the path.

Soon they reached the shore again. Then they rode on until noon without adventure, other than Elias' blunderingly letting his horse get loose when they had stopped for a few minutes to explore some caves hollowed in the sandstone cliffs above the path—caves that would make fine lurking-places for robbers, and very likely in their time were so used. After a rough chase the horse was cornered and captured.

They rode till noon. Then they reached a pleasant camping-place under a tree near the double-arched bridge over the Litany. It was a beautiful picture that lay before them. There was a glimpse of water, the "eye of any landscape," the stone bridge, picturesque against a background of hills, a large khan in the distance, and open meadow-land between, with here and there cows and goats grazing over it. Very soon the travellers' horses, unsaddled and hobbled, were added to the picture, feeding contentedly in the foreground.

Resting there under the trees, Will and Harry were in no haste to resume the journey. They waited an hour or two, then ordered the horses, and Will said as they mounted,

"Come, Harry, we will ride on while Elias and Hassan are packing the saddle-bags. They will overtake us at the bridge, where we will stop to water the horses."

As they approached the bridge they turned down to the right towards the sandy edge of the stream. All at once they heard a great shouting behind them. Looking back they saw their two men hurrying towards them, shouting and beckoning with all their might.

"What is it all about?" said Harry. "They seem to be signing for us to run; but that would be to ride right into the river, where there seems to be no trace at all of a ford."

Will laughed. "No," he said, "the sign means to stop; though no wonder you thought they meant for us to go forward, waving their hands that way with the palms towards us. But what they want of us in such a hurry I don't know. We will wait and find what the trouble is."

The trouble proved to be wholly imaginary. Will laughed again as the excited men came up and explained.

"Harry," he said, "when they saw us turn towards the river they thought we were going to try and wade across. They knew the water was too deep for that, and it is likely there are quicksands besides; so they made those signs—doing what would have been just the thing to send us forward if I had not known that what with us means, 'Go ahead,' with them means, 'Stop.' Now we will let the horses drink; then we will go on over the bridge."

A few hours more of riding and they came in sight of Tyre. Before them was a smooth sweep of white sand, curving around without a break to the little village which is the poor descendant of the old "Island Queen of the Mediterranean."

Elias, ashamed of his failure of the evening before to find lodgings in Sidon, had galloped ahead to make inquiries before the others should arrive. Hassan was lagging behind with the pack-horse. So Will and Harry rode alone in the evening stillness, silent themselves for a while, impressed most deeply with thoughts of what had been there in the past and of what was around them now. The ocean and the mountains and the sky—they were the same, and they alone. All else was changed.

"Harry," said Will, "often as we have thought about Tyre, how different this seeing of it makes the whole history seem—so much more real and vivid."

"Yes, indeed."

"Its secular history and its sacred history too. The Saviour's home in Nazareth, you know, was only some thirty miles away by the shortest route. Christ may often have been on these coasts. We know he once was.* When the disciples were scattered abroad by persecution, after the stoning of Stephen, some of them came here.† And Paul, you know, was here on his last journey to Jerusalem. He remained seven days with the disciples.‡ Luke tells how lovingly they took leave of him at the end of that time—all coming

* Matt. 15:21.   † Acts 11:19.   ‡ Acts 21:4.

TYRE.

out from the city a little way, and when they must separate, kneeling down to pray together on the 'smooth shore.'* Not on a rocky shore, but where it was smooth, just as it is here where we are riding now."

As they came nearer the town Will asked Harry if he saw any sign that the place was once an island, or any sign that they were riding now where Alexander the Great built his causeway through the water, connecting the island and the mainland, so that his troops might have a way to advance and storm the walls.

"There is n't the least sign that I can see of anything of the sort," said Harry. "There is no difference in the beach, excepting that here it curves out more sharply, making a sort of bay; and we can see too across the sand-hills to another bay of the same sort on the other side."

"Yet when Alexander came, three hundred years before the time of Christ, this was all open water. The island lay half a mile from the mainland, and the water was eighteen feet deep in the channel between. The Tyrians seem to have thought their city was impregnable. The water protected it; and, besides, they had walls that, on the land side, were one hundred and fifty feet high. It took Alexander seven months to cap-

* Acts 21 : 5 (αἰγιαλὸν—a smooth shore).

ture the place. He built his causeway of timber from the Lebanon forests, and of stone that he found in the ruins of that part of Tyre which had once existed on the mainland. That accounts to some extent for there being no signs now of what was very likely once the largest part of Tyre, though never the strongest part. One almost completed causeway the Tyrians destroyed. But at once Alexander began another that was larger still, and he pushed it through till it reached the walls. Then there was fierce hand-to-hand fighting. Both sides were well equipped with munitions of war—stones, javelins, bows, battering-rams. One novel means of defence the besieged used effectively. They brought hot sand from their furnaces and used it as boiling oil was often used. When the attacking columns rushed forward to scale the walls they rained the fine sand down upon them. It penetrated under their armor and was like fire against their flesh. After a long siege the place was captured. Eight thousand of the citizens were slain; three thousand were sold as slaves. Ever since, for two thousand years, the wind and the sea have been drifting the sand over the causeway, until it is all as you see it now."

By this time they had reached the entrance to the town. Elias met them. He had found the lodging-place to which the friends in Sidon had directed them, and had learned that they could be accommodated there.

They were guided through the narrow streets, between high-walled houses and yards. Few people met them, and of those few it was sad to see how large a proportion were crippled in one way or another, most of them by entire or partial blindness. It was a dead, poverty-stricken, ruinous place.

"How forlorn and miserable everything seems!" said Harry.

They came to the port. One narrow pier reached out a few rods into deep water. Looking over the edge they could see that it was made in part of carefully finished columns and foundation stones that must once have been portions of beautiful temples or palaces. A few small boats were drawn up to the shore.

"And this," said Will, "is all that is left of the city whose fleets once sailed to all parts of the known world and ruled the Mediterranean: a city which founded colonies like that of Carthage; which could hardly be mastered by the greatest conquerors of the world—withstood Nebuchadnezzar for thirteen years, and it is not certain that he conquered then—which was great in the time of David and Solomon; which was called a strong city* when it first appears in history; whose age no one knows."

"How long has the place been as it is now?" asked Harry. "It must have had hard fortune again since those worst times, for it was well off in the time of Christ."

"Yes; it recovered gradually from the blow Alexander gave it, and in the time of the Romans was very prosperous again. Much of its wealth was due to its dyes of Tyrian purple, made from a shell-fish of the genus Murex. It was still prosperous in the time of the Crusaders.† One of the greatest of the Crusaders was buried here—Frederick Barbarossa. The fatal day for Tyre, which left her much as we see her now, came 150 years later.‡ At that time the Sultan of Egypt and Damascus was besieging Acre. After two months the city was captured. Then the Tyrians knew that their turn would come next, and they knew too what their fate would be if they resisted. Almost to a man they left the city. The next day when the Saracens came they found it forsaken. They entered and sacked it unopposed. It never has recovered from that disaster, and probably never will. Though it has gained somewhat of late years, the prophecy in Ezekiel has been literal-

---

* Josh. 19 : 29.   † Tyre surrendered to the Crusaders in 1124.   ‡ 1291.

ly fulfilled which describes its site as a place left desolate, where fishermen dwell, and spread their nets on the lonely rocks.* But come, it is time to find what our quarters are to be for the night."

They were guided a few steps farther through the streets to a private house belonging to one of the native Christians—a teacher. They entered by a gateway through a high wall to an inner yard, from which a stairway led to the dwelling-rooms in the second story. There they were received by the members of the family. The place was much above the average, compared with the houses about it. There seemed to be even some degree of comfort.

It was a good opportunity, they thought, to find how the better class of natives lived. So when Elias came and asked what arrangement they wished to make for supper, Will told him to request their host to provide the supper, and to let it be simply such native dishes as they were accustomed to use. The room where they sat, and where they were to sleep, was furnished for the most part in European style; but around the sides there were continuous lounges. Upon these their beds were afterwards spread.

* Ezek. 26:14. Writing in 1697, Maundrell says of it, "Its present inhabitants are only a few poor wretches that harbor in vaults and subsist upon fishing." Hasselquist (1766) says, "Here are about ten inhabitants, who live by fishing."

By the time supper was served the travellers were thoroughly hungry. They came to the table, furnished also, though rather sparingly, with cutlery and crockery of English make, ready to do all possible justice to whatever was set before them. As they took their seats, however, the prospect for an enjoyable meal was poor, excepting for their unusual appetites. But they hoped that things would taste better than they looked.

"Harry, help yourself to the bread," said Will.

"You must mean this. But I wouldn't think so, excepting that it looks less unlike bread than anything else on the table," remarked Harry, as he carefully tore a piece from one of a pile of thin brown cakes. "They are like home griddle-cakes in size and thickness. I wonder what they taste like."

"Taste and see," said Will.

Harry did so, guardedly. He quietly laid aside what was left.

"It is the native bread," said Will, "such as the people always use. If only it was salted a little, and was brought crisp from the fire, it would be much more palatable. But oftenest the meal is simply mixed with water and baked in large batches over the coals or on hot stones."

"If there was butter, or something of the sort,

to go with it," said Harry, "I could eat it possibly. What is that, I wonder? It looks as though it might be good. It looks like nice rich cream. Please give me a little with the bread."

"Yes, this is something wholesome; and it is a standard dish, with those who can afford it, all through the country. It is curdled goats' milk."

"Is it? I'm glad of that. I've heard of it often; now I will know how it tastes. I hope it is as good as it looks."

Harry was encouraged, and helped himself bountifully; but at the first taste,

"Bah!" he exclaimed, "it is like sour milk."

"Well," said Will, "our hosts have been extravagant in their desire to favor us. Here are two other more substantial dishes, and such, certainly, as we have never seen at home. What one of them is I cannot guess. And the other I know only because I once saw a dish like it in Constantinople. We will try this unknown something first. It looks as much like boiled cucumbers as anything."

"And it tastes like them!" exclaimed Harry, "tastes as I imagine they would, as near like them as any known thing in America can. And they are stuffed with something—with rice. Cousin Will, I'll thank you for a very little bit of the—the forlorn hope, the last dish on the bill of fare."

This proved to be the least unpalatable of the whole, but still a few mouthfuls were all they could eat of it. It consisted of little balls of rice wrapped snugly in pickled grape-leaves and then fried.

"I am glad to know what the better class of natives consider luxuries," said Will; "but it is fortunate that we have something different in our saddle-bags, left over from lunch, else we would have to go hungry to bed. Wont you find Elias and ask him to bring the bread, honey, eggs, and oranges."

"Yes, I will, and very gladly," said Harry.

So finally they made a comfortable meal. After it, as they left the table, Harry remarked,

"And besides all that was on the table which was peculiar, underneath it the whole time the fleas about my legs were—well, worse."

They were weary with the long day. They sat for a while in the twilight, then were ready for rest.

The next day was the Sabbath. Most of it they spent on the seashore. They could feel themselves much nearer to God there than anywhere in the town. In the afternoon they found the ruins of what was once a beautiful Christian church, where some of the early church fathers are supposed to have preached, and where doubtless the crusaders met to worship during the years in which they held the city.

Then they roamed on again towards another part of the sea. They crossed an open field scattered with graves, where the monuments were low, rectangular piles of flat stones. Among the tombs two little girls came hurrying, the one leading the other by the hand. The younger one was blind, and they came to beg.

Reaching the shore, they found that it rose there in bold rocky cliffs far above the water. Where the height overlooks a low, black reef that the waves break against and race over, sometimes in foam and sometimes in dark currents, and where there were fishermen working on the rocks below mending their nets, they sat waiting in the beautiful deepening twilight until the night should be fully come. It was dark when they found their way back to the town.

CHAPTER XIX.

TYRE TO ACRE.

At half-past six the travellers were in the saddle, as fresh for the day's ride as if it was the first morning of their journeying instead of the third. And there was good need of an early and fresh start. The work before them would make the day a hard one.

"We must reach Haifa to-night," said Will, "and Haifa is thirty-six miles away. The men want to take two days for it, not because it is too far, but because they generally do so, and because it is gain for them to keep us on the way as long as possible. No doubt though that the ride will be a severe one. The way is long, and parts of the road are very bad."

"It could hardly be rougher than we have had already."

"No, but the badness is not in the roughness. It is in the steepness. There are bold spurs of the mountains between here and Acre, two of which are especially noted. They strike across from the main range, not almost to the sea, but quite to it, into it. There is not even a narrow passage-way along their bases, as there is, for instance, between Mount Carmel and the water, but one must clamber over them as he best can, by paths that need sure-footed horses for safe crossing. The first of the promontories with its cliffs of white limestone shows there very plainly before us now, though it is two hours away. Those cliffs give it its name, 'The White Promontory.' There is another similar promontory six miles farther south, formerly called 'The Ladder of Tyre.'"

For two hours from Tyre they followed the curves of the shore. Then the rocks made a great wall before them. They turned a few rods inland and began the slow ascent. Soon the path wound to the very face of the cliff, high over the water. There was no other course for it to take, and there was no passing there excepting as a way was cut in the perpendicular rock. In and out the path wound. Sometimes it was so steep and smooth that steps were cut for the horses' hoofs. It was much like climbing a ladder. They were two hundred feet straight up above the waves, which they could see, but scarcely hear, foaming over the flat, black reefs below. If they had taken one of the flint stones with which the white rock is dotted and lined, and reaching over had dropped it, it would hardly have touched anything until it reached the foam; and at every rod as they passed on the grouping of the reefs and the masses of white water at the base of the cliffs gave new pictures. There was constant change. It was a wild place.

That was in the foreground, but when they raised their eyes and looked beyond, back towards Tyre, there was the fairest distant view, by far, of anything they had yet seen along the coast. It was their last view of Tyre, lying beautiful now in a soft haze far away towards the horizon, and with the shining sea between. The descent began. It seemed steeper than the ascent, and it grew steeper and steeper.

"Cousin Will," said Harry at last, "I am going to dismount. This is altogether too suggestive of unintended somersets for horse and rider. To say nothing of the danger, I don't think we would look well rolling down this slope, for if we got a good start we should have to roll from top to bottom, it is so steep."

He dismounted and walked the rest of the way. He led his horse, but was careful to keep to one side, out of the way in case he fell. They reached the foot of the pass in safety, and came again to a comparatively level path. As they rode Harry exclaimed,

"Why, we are travelling by the side of what seems to be a paved road!"

"It is that," said Will. "The remains of what were most likely military roads are not uncommon in Syria, and this was one of the chief of them. The route that we are following now has always been the highway of armies. Alexander's camp was located near here, according to tradition, when he was planning his attack on Tyre."

Two hours farther on they came to the last ridge, "Râs en Nakûrah," the old "Ladder of Tyre." It is higher than the others, but the path is not as steep as that over the "White Promontory." It curves about, leading gradually upward towards an old tower that marks the summit of the ridge. There, suddenly, without the slightest previous sign of what was coming, the new view to the south opened before them. It was startling in its suddenness and its greatness. From the point where they stood the mountain falls away, almost perpendicularly for some hundreds of feet, down to an immense plain, which stretches off smooth, seemingly, as a floor, to a dim line of far mountains in the south, which they knew must be the range of Carmel, and in front of which, too far away to be easily distinguished, lies the city of Acre.

It was the great "Plain of Acre," fertile as a garden, covered with fields of grain and pasture-land and clumps of trees, dotted over with flocks of sheep and goats and droves of cattle as far as the eye could reach. To the east lines of decreasing hills bounded their view. The sea lay on the west.

It was hardly as beautiful perhaps, this first view of the Plain of Acre, as their last view of Tyre had been a few hours before; but it was more striking, the sudden effect was more thrilling, all was larger, grander.

"Can we not noon here?" said Harry. "It is too splendid to leave, and we are so far up towards the sky it is cool and pleasant for resting."

"I wish we could stay," answered Will, "for this is another of the views that one wants never to forget, one of the places where we seem lifted up nearer to God. But there is no safe place here for the horses, neither is there any grass or water. We will wait, though, while the men go on down to the foot of the pass. They can prepare the camp there, and we will follow at our leisure."

The afternoon ride was as different as it well could be from that of the morning. It was through a rich farming region, over soft and easy paths, instead of up and down rock-stairs.

It was growing late as they neared Acre, and Haifa is nearly three hours beyond Acre. Several times since morning Elias had spoken of the desirableness of shortening the day's journey and stopping for the night in Acre or near it. Moreover, he and Hassan had evidently been delaying as much as possible all the afternoon. Now Elias referred to the matter again, indirectly, praising the attractiveness of a neighboring village as a lodging-place. Plainly there was a tendency towards rebellion.

Will answered shortly that they would lodge that night at Haifa. "And we must explore Acre besides," he said; "there is no time to lose."

With that he and Harry rode on at the gallop, scarcely looking behind again in their interest in what they were passing and approaching. There before them was the strongly fortified city of Acre, which had been a strong city in the days of the Judges,* and has been strong through all the centuries since, and is strong to-day.

The city seemed to them to be built on a natural rise of ground, close to the sea. But that was a mistake. The seeming hill was only the ruins of the old Acres that had lived and died in long succession since the first Acre was founded there thousands of years ago: just how many years ago no one knows. On every side of this

* Judges 1:31. It is mentioned also in Acts 21:7, and frequently in the books of the Apocrypha, under its other name of Ptolemais.

mound, excepting towards the sea, there was an almost perfectly open and level country, crossed by frequent roads and by the ruins of an ancient aqueduct. Since the beginning of the Christian era Acre has been captured by the Arabs, by the Genoese, by Sultan Saladin, by the Crusaders, by the Egyptians, by the Turks, by the Egyptians again, and finally, in 1840, by an allied English, Turkish, and Austrian fleet. It was one of the most important of the strongholds of the Crusaders, and the last that was yielded by them before they were driven wholly out of Syria. And still it was strong enough in 1799 to resist the French under Napoleon. He tried for sixty-one days to capture it, and failed. It is a strictly military city. There are no houses outside the walls. It is garrisoned. The one gate is closed at sundown.

The path led the two riders under an arch of the aqueduct, then turned sharply to the right towards the city. As they checked their horses they looked back. Elias and Hassan were nowhere in sight.

"Why, where can the men be?" exclaimed Harry.

"We have come rather fast for Hassan with the baggage-horse," said Will; "but Elias could easily have kept at least in sight. We will go on. Most likely he will appear soon from behind that line of trees."

Now and then they looked back, expecting each time to see one or both of the men; but there was no sign of them.

Will was growing stern. "There may be some accident," he said. "It looks, though, as if they were plotting to force us to stay here all night."

By this time they had reached the gate of the city. But they could not enter without running the risk of more delay by missing the men when they should finally arrive. Late as it was, the only way was to wait for them outside. So they waited, walking their horses back and forth, sometimes dismounting for a change and leading them.

Loungers gathered about, seeing that something was wrong, but unable to ask or to understand what it was. They could have had no doubt though that Will was very angry at something or somebody.

It was nearly sunset before the men appeared together in the distance, moving very leisurely along towards the place where they were waiting. As they came up Will accosted Elias. Hassan knew hardly a word of English.

"Well, what do you mean by this?"

"By what, sir?" said Elias innocently.

"Tell me what you mean by this! What have you to say for yourself?"

"Hassan would n't take the saddle-bags, sir; and I could n't gallop after you with them."

"You could have done it as easily as you galloped after that fox yesterday with the saddle-bags. But Hassan would have taken them; and if he would not, you could have walked your horse twice as fast as you did."

"We thought there was time enough."

"Time for what?"

"To reach Acre. We can't go any farther than here to-night. We made no agreement to do it."

"You did, a written agreement; and you will keep it!"

"If it says that we would go in one day from Tyre to Haifa, we did not know it, sir."

"You either knew it, or lied in pretending to understand English when I told you. And as for Hassan, the paper was translated for him. Now I know what you have been plotting and lagging for all day. Have you more excuses?"

"We can't do it, sir. Hassan wont."

"Hassan will, and so will you. Give me those saddle-bags, man, quick!"

Elias unfastened them and handed them over

to Will. He took them and threw them over the pack-horse.

"Hassan, Haifa, go!" he said, pointing down the beach.

And Hassan went without delay.

"Now do you guide us through Acre—unless you have lied again in saying you know the way."

Elias turned submissively and led the way into the city.

They entered by the massive gate, and explored, as rapidly as possible, the market-place, where the merchants were sitting with their wares on the pavements, so closely that it was hard to avoid riding over them and their customers. They explored the narrow streets, bordered with massive and, in places, ruined stone-work, and the dungeons, and a pretty mosque near by, with a courtway paved in rich mosaic, and with a fountain in the centre, and flowers and shrubs and trees. All that there was of interest they saw.

CHAPTER XX.

A NIGHT RIDE TO HAIFA.

They repassed the gateway. As they left the city and rode down towards the wide beach a very pretty picture was before them. It was the pleasantest hour of the day after the noon-time heat, and many towns-people had come out to enjoy it on the shore, old and young together, men, women and children, dressed in bright garments and with happy faces, standing in groups, or walking and playing by the water. It was like a festival time. But it was only the pleasant daily festival time of the people for rest and gossip.

Suddenly Elias struck his horse with his whip and dashed off through the crowd of people down the beach. In an instant the other horses were on the run, excited and unmanageable, eager to overtake their comrade. For a while they were wholly beyond control. There was no stopping them. All that the riders could do was to keep their seats and try to guide their horses. It was terrible for a moment. It seemed scarcely possible that no one would be injured, as they rushed among the children and the men and women.

But it was quickly over. The crowd was behind them, and the open beach, smooth and hard as a floor, before them. The two horses flew over it; but the danger was past now. All that was needed was to keep a steady pressure on the bits. They would soon yield. In a few minutes they were walking quietly side by side.

"I think it is excusable for us to look pale after that," said Will. "There was a group of three or four people straight in front of my horse. I thought they would be under his hoofs. I tried to turn, and I suppose I did, but my foot must almost have struck them as I swept by. I expected to hear a scream. How many there were, and which of them was nearest, I don't know. All I know is that one of them was a little child."

Some two miles from Acre they came to the river Belus, and forded it where it winds through the sand and empties into the sea. It is dignified with the name of "river," but in reality is hardly more than a brook rising in a large marsh six miles away.

Then for miles they rode around the curve of the beautiful bay alone, for Hassan and Elias were out of sight in advance. The city grew dim behind them, and the white houses of Haifa and the outline of Mount Carmel against the sky were dim before them. The sun had sunk below the horizon in the west, and the full moon had risen from the plain on their left. The wind had died away. There were waves along the shore, but they were not boisterous; they only whispered. The west faded until the stars came out and the night was as dark as it could be with so fair a moon hung low in so cloudless a sky. It was weirdly beautiful.

"I imagine," said Will, "that when we look back on this night ride around the Bay of Acre, it will be one of the times that we would be least willing of all to forget."

In places they walked their horses. Sometimes they rode side by side at full speed, galloping close by the line of breaking waves where the wet sand muffled the sound of the horses' hoofs. Sometimes, for a rest, they would dismount and walk, leading their horses, with the bridles over their arms.

Once, as they walked thus, they saw a delicate white shell resting on the sand, as though it had just been laid there, very softly, by the falling tide. Harry picked it up. It was nearly perfect; there was no flaw excepting a slight bruise on the tinted lip.

"Good!" exclaimed Will; "that is the murex, the *Murex trunculus*, which I have been wishing we could find ever since we left Tyre."

"Is it the kind they made the 'Tyrian purple' from?"

"Yes."

"I am going to carry this little shell home with me as a relic, and a reminder of our ride to-night. Wouldn't you?"

"Yes; it will have a double interest."

Harry pocketed it carefully. They mounted and galloped on again.

"Do you know," said Will, "a few years ago we could not have been here at this time of night with any sort of safety. I suppose there has been more robbing of travellers in this region than almost anywhere else in Palestine."

"Do you suppose there is any risk?"

"Not much, if any; only enough at the most to add a trifle to the excitement. But after to-day, we shall be likely enough any time to meet wandering Bedouins. They come in from beyond the Jordan by way of the Plain of Esdraelon. They used to come often at harvest-time in large bands and ravage the whole country. But that seldom happens now. Usually they are as harmless as the travellers whom they meet, though no doubt they would be glad to rob them if they dared."

A little farther on and they drew near the mouth of the Kishon. They had overtaken and passed their men a short way back.

"This is quite a river," Harry said as they came in sight of it. "Can we cross it safely?"

"Yes; but not in the narrowest part. There is always a sand-bar across the mouth, and by following that and holding our feet well up on the horses' sides we will escape a wetting. In the summer, when the water is low and the west winds are strong, the bar conquers the river and bridges it wholly. Then the little water that is running sinks under the sand, and one can cross on foot. But in the rainy season men can cross only in boats, and horses have to swim. There is danger too from quicksands. The river was swollen like that in the Old Testament time when it bore so important a part in the destruction of Sisera's army, after its defeat by the Israelites under Deborah and Barak.* Sisera was encamped on the Plain of Esdraelon between the Kishon and the mountains of Samaria. By Deborah's directions Barak marched from Mount Tabor with his ten thousand men and attacked the enemy fiercely, surprising and defeating them. Then he pursued them down the plain towards their strongholds located in the pass a few miles

* Judges 5:21.

southeast of Haifa. The mountain on one side and the marshes of Thora with the Kishon on the other shut them in more and more closely. Very soon the mountain and the river touched in front of them. There was no escape. And yet just beyond rose their strong castle of Harosheth. If only they could have gained that they would have been safe. Those who were behind pressed upon the ranks in front. Horses and chariots and horsemen and footmen were driven into the water. Those who were not slain by the sword the river destroyed. None escaped. But where there was then such a raging river now it is likely we shall find hardly a sign of water. In the dry season the whole upper part of the Kishon disappears; and running water is found only between this point on the beach and a place three miles inland, where there are large constant springs."

They reached the fording-place. Under the moonlight the water looked very beautiful. It was wider and rougher than they had expected, and by the line of the waves they knew that the ford led, not straight across, but in a curve far to the right out into the bay. But they had no thought of risk.

"Come on, Harry!" and Will touched his horse with the spurs. The horse was afraid and tried to draw back, but he forced him in. Harry followed.

The water only very gradually deepened—but it deepened surely—to the horses' fetlocks, to their knees, to their bellies; and they were not yet half way across. There was a strong current, and the wind against it raised a sea that began to make their horses stagger. Neither was it easy now to be certain of the direction: they could judge only by the roughness of the waves; a few feet either side and they would be in deep water. And now the water was well up on the horses' shoulders. It would not do to risk letting them swim here, unless they had to; the current was too strong and they were too far out.

But at last they were on a level, and seemingly rather more than half way across. Just then Will happened to glance seaward, and there, whether because they were in a more exposed place or because the wind had really risen, behold, was a great wave rushing towards them that would surely sweep their horses. If others were following it they certainly were in great danger. Will forgot all about himself.

"Harry, quick, you are too far in; pull to the right!" he shouted; and then again, as he saw the wave almost upon them; "It's too late; cling to your horse!"

He wheeled his own just in time to make a stride or two towards Harry and then to face the wave. It drenched him and he felt his horse lose its footing; but only for a moment; then he stood firm again. He dashed the water out of his hair and eyes. There was terrible fear in his heart. There was Harry to the east of him clinging to his horse, and not far away; but the horse was swimming with only his head and floating mane out of the water, and swimming the wrong way— up the river towards still deeper water and quicksands beyond.

"Harry, drop out of the saddle, else you'll drown your horse, but cling to him! Now try and turn him! Keep cool and save your breath in case you have to swim."

Would the horse turn? It seemed not. He was frightened and confused! Will was just ready to take the last chance, and a desperate one; he had thrown off his coat and in a minute would have been swimming after them, when the horse yielded and turned towards him.

"Now, Harry, hold as lightly as you can with one hand and try to swim with the other! A minute more, Harry; I can almost reach you."

But he would never have reached him, though now he was almost within arms-length. The horse was trying again to turn towards the land,

and Harry had no strength to hinder him. Will saw his hold loosening.

"I can't do it, Cousin Will."

In an instant Will spurred his horse a little nearer, slipped the long bridle over his head, and was in the water. A few strokes and he could just reach Harry and his horse. It was hard work for a minute; then he had them safe; both horses stood firm. He helped Harry into his saddle and regained his own.

The waves were still running high, but the worst of it was over. Close together they went carefully on. The water shoaled rapidly—to the horses' knees, to their fetlocks. They were safe again on the dry land.

They looked back over the beautiful moon-lit water out of which they were escaped. It had been a sudden, wholly unanticipated danger. It seemed unreal, except for their dripping clothes. They said nothing; only a word from Will:

"'When thou passest through the waters, I will be with thee; and through the rivers, they shall not overflow thee.' It is true literally for us, Harry."

When they had seen their men come up and get safely through the now quieter water, they turned away and rode hard towards Haifa. It was late when they reached the town, but they found comfortable accommodations at an inn in the German quarter.

The ride had been long and full of excitement; yet, when they had rested a little, they found that although tired, they were not "tired out." It was a comfortable, hungry and sleepy tiredness, Harry said. But the men fared worse. It was so late Hassan had trouble in finding food and lodging for his horses, and Elias had succumbed to the night-riding and was down with chills.

"I am sorry for them," Harry said; "but it is all their own fault."

"They have had a needed lesson," Will said. "They are not likely to rebel again. The only safe way was to be decided with them at the first."

Just as they were finishing supper Elias came into the room and said meekly to Will that Hassan wished to see him.

"Let him come in," said Will.

Hassan entered.

"Well, what do you want?"

Elias explained that he wanted the first payment for the horses.

"What was the bargain in regard to that?"

"That you were to pay us on the fourth day, sir, from Beirût."

"And here at Haifa?"

"Yes, sir."

"But you have been pretending that the agreement was to go no farther than Acre on the fourth day. You can hardly claim now that I was wrong in saying that you two were plotting and lying."

Will paid them and sent them off. He and Harry went to their rooms and to their beds, which Harry, upon inspection, reported to be remarkably free from the Eastern pest of fleas, clean and comfortable. In about two minutes they were sound asleep.

CHAPTER XXI.

HAIFA TO NAZARETH.

"WE have an easy ride before us to-day," said Will, "across the hills to Nazareth. There will be time enough if we leave here by nine or ten. So we can take till that hour for our excursion to Mount Carmel. We will start at once."

"Do we want the men?"

"Hassan must go to take care of the horses. Elias may as well stay here till we return."

Leaving the inn, they followed an easy path through the pleasant German settlement, through silvery old olive-orchards on the lower slopes of the mount, up a steeper, but still easy path six hundred feet to the summit.

At an old monastery there they were received by the monks and ushered into the waiting-room of the establishment. They were thirsty after the ride, and a pleasant drink was brought them by one of the brethren, made from some preparation of the juice of oranges. It was offered voluntarily, without request on their part. Then they were urged to allow breakfast to be prepared, and could scarcely excuse themselves with the answer that they had already eaten. After resting they were taken through the convent, and, at last, out upon its high, flat roof for the fine view of hills and plains and of the "Great Sea" to the west.

"I wish," said Harry, "that we could have spent last night here, everything and everybody seem so pleasant."

"Yes," answered Will. "But it would have been doing too much to have tried to reach here yesterday evening. It would have been the last straw on the camel's back. Had you supposed that Mount Carmel was as long a mountain as it is? As we saw it yesterday, and have seen it this morning, it stretches away in a ridge twelve miles long, I should think, towards the hills of Samaria in the southeast. And it was near that end, not here, that the prophets of Baal assembled when Elijah called them together to prove by the test of fire whether Baal or Jehovah was the true God."*

They left the roof of the convent, said good-by to the friendly monks, and were ready for the return. Hassan brought the horses, but Harry proposed that they walk part way down; he wanted to explore a cave which they had seen while ascending, by the roadside in the limestone rock.

* 1 Kings 18:19 ff.

"For aught we know," said Harry, "it may sometimes have sheltered Elijah and Elisha."

Will assented. They walked as far as the cave. Then they mounted and were soon back at the inn. Elias joined them, and they rode towards Nazareth.

The route led for some miles along the base of Carmel and across the Plain of Acre towards the entrance between the hills to the Plain of Esdraelon. They passed the large fountains of the Kishon, and a little farther on crossed the nearly dry bed of the stream, finding their way among thick clumps of blossoming oleander-bushes. There was no running water, only still pools, with a flock of goats among them and an Arab boy for keeper.

They met many travellers. It was a much frequented way along which they were journeying. There were farmers, shepherds, traders, on foot and mounted, groups of evil-visaged Arabs. Once a finely-mounted Bedouin rode by, armed with a gun and sword and long, slim lance. They passed a migrating family. The three children were mounted on a diminutive donkey. The women wore head-dresses of copper coins, strung loosely together and laid over their foreheads and hair.

At one point, where the road forked, there was

a dispute between Elias and Hassan as to which was the path they ought to take. Elias, as guide, had his way, and they kept to the right hand.

But Elias was wrong, as he soon found. Then, instead of retracing their steps, they struck across through the growing wheat, that reached already to their horses' heads, towards the other path where it led to the north, up into the beautiful hill-country of Galilee.

Now the scenery differed greatly from anything they had before found. They had left the sea and the plain behind them, though from time to time they had distant glimpses of the latter.

One new feature in the landscape showed itself before they had reached the summit of the first steep hill. They had seen scarcely a single fine tree, other than cultivated ones, since leaving Beirût. Now they were riding through splendid groves of oaks.

"We must lunch under one of these great trees," said Will.

"There are as fine ones, sir," said Elias, "and there is a better view, just beyond at the top of the hill."

"Very well, we will stop there."

It was a noble tree which they finally chose as the green tent for their noon camp. The branches hung low and thick and sheltered them thoroughly from the hot sun, and the heat was tempered besides by a cool breeze from the north. They spread their blankets over the grass and wild flowers. Elias brought the lunch.

When they had eaten, they read for a while, wrote, transferred the flowers which they had found to their pocket-press,* talked over their plans, lying there at their ease under the green roof, on the green floor, near the breezy summit of this first of the hills of Galilee. So they rested for an hour or more.

The afternoon ride was very varied—up and down hills, across inlying spurs from the Plain of Esdraelon covered with ripening grain, into deep valleys, over high plateaus, but all the time gradually ascending. Across one of these plateaus they had their first view of Mount Tabor. It seemed to lie like a great, black half-moon just beyond the edge of the plain. The impression was of a much larger, more imposing mountain than they had imagined.

In and out, among the hills and over them, the path wound. It was lonelier and wilder than the way along the plain had been. Wild pigeons often flew up before them from clumps of bushes and the shelter of rocks and grass. Elias

---

* They carried a miniature flower-press in which they kept what Harry called a " flower journal."

wasted his powder and shot, and tried Will's patience, in vain efforts to shoot them. There were seldom any other birds or any animals in sight, but of insects there were many. The ants interested them. Often they rode over armies of them whose lines of march crossed the beaten footpath between the grain-fields. They were plundering the fields. Each ant as they marched was heavily laden with its burden of food, its grain of wheat. The busy multitudes reminded them of Solomon's advice to the sluggard.*

And now they were approaching very near to Nazareth. There were more signs of inhabitants above them. Below, to their right, on the slope of the hill stood a substantial stone house in the midst of vineyards and silvery olive-orchards, and here and there were less extensive establishments. A few rods farther on, up the steep part to the ridge of the next line of hills—what would they see there? Simply a common Syrian town? No. They reached the summit, and there below them lay Nazareth! Nazareth, a little Syrian town; yes; but ah, how far from seeming commonplace! Dear indeed it has been to the thoughts of millions of little children, and of the middle-aged and the old. Nazareth, where the Christ-child dwelt with Mary and Joseph, and where he in-

* Prov. 6:6.

NAZARETH.

creased in wisdom and stature and in favor with God and man, and whence at last he went out to finish the work which has redeemed the world.

> Nazareth! home of Mary mild,
> Home of Jesus, Saviour-child,
> Quiet lie among your hills,
> Speak no word; your honor fills
> All the world, and ever will
> While the world through vale and hill
> Humbly worship Mary's child,
> Jesus, Saviour, meek and mild.
>
> Let your maidens, if they will,
> At your fount their pitchers fill;
> All the world will draw from thee
> Better water flowing free;
> Let your maidens softly sing
> Round your ever-flowing spring;
> Softest words and water's flow
> Can but echo as they go,
> "Nazareth's Jesus now is King,
> Jesus, Saviour, him we sing."
>
> Nazareth! home of God's own child,
> Home of Mary pure and mild,
> No proud scribes need now to show
> Whether good from you can go;
> Tiny sparrows, nothing worth,
> Lilies fading from their birth,
> Tell of him whom Nazareth gave,
> Tell of Jesus, strong to save.
> Jesus, Saviour, gracious King!
> All the world their praises bring.

The steep hillside covered by its clinging houses, and the valley, and the encircling hills with their far-off views, and the precipice over which the towns-people would once have cast the Saviour, all are the same now as they were eighteen hundred years ago. The stage is the same. Only the actors upon it are changed.

"It will shorten the distance to the hospice, sir," said Elias, "if we keep right down the hill between the houses instead of going around."

"Take the shortest way, if you can get the horses down there. It looks to me too steep for them."

"It is steep, sir, and very dusty; but Hassan and I will lead them."

They all dismounted. Will and Harry followed behind, while the horses with the men scrambled and slid and stumbled down the narrow streets, through clouds of white dust, to the comparatively level streets below. There they remounted, and after riding a few rods farther, reached the spacious Franciscan hospice, where they hoped to find quarters for the night.

"This looks comfortable from the outside," said Harry, as they waited for an answer to their knock. "I wonder what it is inside."

"And the place is strong enough," said Will, "with its heavy doors and few windows and stone walls, to be a small fortress. Likely enough it has had to serve as such in its time."

The bolts were drawn and the door swung

open. In the doorway stood a monk, round-faced and stout, with tonsured head and full beard. He wore a brown dress of coarse serge, cowled, girded at the waist with a cord, and reaching to the feet. It was "Fra Johannes" in the costume of his order. He and Elias conferred together.

"Is n't he jolly-looking?" remarked Harry. "No fear but he will take good care of us. I do n't believe he lives on sour milk and pickled grape-leaves and boiled cucumbers!"

"What does he say, Elias?"

"He says that you are welcome, sir, and will you dismount and go in?"

Worthy Fra Johannes! He received them at the door, and conducted them first to the long, dimly-lighted dining-room. There he placed refreshments before them, to serve, he said, until a heartier meal could be provided. Then he showed them to their room.

"Well, this is more promising for comfort than anything we have seen in a good while," said Will.

"Is n't it though! It's a real clean, cosey little room."

"And what a busy market-place the window overlooks. Riders and footmen are passing. Merchants are there with their wares. Really this seems to be quite a stirring town."

"And if there isn't a blacksmith too, with his shop right in the street, there by the wall! two of them, sitting on the ground with their stock in trade by them—hammers, nails, and horseshoes. It's certainly convenient for their customers. There's a horseman, now, stopping to have his horse shod."

Across the street behind a high stone wall were other buildings of the Franciscans, their convent and the Church of the Annunciation with its spires rising against the sky.

"I suppose we ought to explore the place before dark, oughtn't we?" said Harry.

"Yes, there will not be much time in the morning. But there is very little I care to see among the so-called sacred places that they show. These stone buildings with their modern traditions do not interest me nearly as much as the place itself, the hills and the valleys that are as they have always been.

"There is one spot though I would not fail to visit, the village fountain, the only one there is here, from which the women and children bring their daily supplies now, just as the women and children of Nazareth, with Mary and Jesus among them, brought theirs in the long-ago Bible times. We will hunt up Brother Johannes and inquire of him about the sights of the place."

They found the good brother. When he understood their errand he at once offered to be their guide. Most of the sacred places, he said, were held by their order; some few were held by the other sects. He took a bunch of great keys and went out before them bareheaded, as is the custom with the brotherhood. Many of the people whom they met as they walked saluted him, especially many of the little children. Some of them kissed his hand and pressed it first to their hearts then to their foreheads. One pretty little girl included Will and Harry in the respectful salutation. They visited the neighboring Church of the Annunciation, built, according to the claim of the priests, on the spot where the angel Gabriel announced to Mary the birth of the Messiah. They were taken down a flight of stairs and shown "Mary's cave" as the exact place of the vision. A dim light is always kept burning there. The guide lighted a candle and led them back of the first cave to another, with a blackened outlet up through the rock to the outside air. This he said was Mary's kitchen. In different parts of the town they were shown the so-called synagogue where Christ read and expounded the Scriptures, and the workshop of Joseph, and a room containing a large flat stone, "the table of Christ and his disciples."

Said Will, "They show us these things with as much confidence as if they did not know that in the beginning of the thirteenth century Nazareth was wholly destroyed by the Saracens—perhaps they do not know it—and that for three or four hundred years after, although the town was partly rebuilt, it was scarcely known to the Christian world. Few pilgrims ever visited the place. It is only of late that the sacred places have been rediscovered or reinvented, and Nazareth restored to something of the favor which it possessed in the sixth and seventh centuries."

"It seems to be a prosperous, lively place now," said Harry; "I mean compared with other villages that we have seen."

"Yes, I suppose there are five or six thousand people living here now. One reason of its growth has been its nearness to the Plain of Esdraelon. Many of the farmers of that region, who would live there if they could be secure from the Bedouins, have their homes here instead."

"Fra Johannes tells me there is one other place he wants us to visit, the 'Chapel of Mary's Well.' It belongs, he says, to the Greek Church, and it is built over the place where Mary used to come to draw water. It is quite at the end of the village."

They reached the little church and found the

interior lighted by dimly-burning lamps. In front of the shrine the attendant stooped and removed the cover from a small, dark hole in the floor, and, lowering a tin cup, brought up water for them to drink. It was from "Mary's Well," he told them.

When they left the chapel the sun was nearly set; but they delayed a few moments longer, for they were close by the public fountain, where the women of the village were coming and going with large earthen water-jars, carried easily on their heads and shoulders. It was a peculiar and suggestive picture; for the customs now of the people cannot be very different from what they were in the time of Mary, and the fountain is the very same. It is now, as it has always been, the "Fountain of Nazareth," though there is modern masonry about it and the water is caught in new-made troughs.

They returned to the hospice. Dinner was ready. They took their places again at the long table and enjoyed thoroughly the well-served food—soup, meat, vegetables, and dessert.

Then they bade Fra Johannes good night and withdrew to their room. But the night outside was too beautiful to leave it wholly for sleep. They sat by the window looking out into the moonlight. They recalled the varied later history of the place: how Napoleon had rested there after defeating the Turks on the plain to the south; what the Saracens had done, and the Crusaders; but they dwelt more than all, and again and again, on the thought that among these hills, under moonlight like this, through pleasant days and days of storm, influenced continually by such surroundings, Christ had dwelt, with Mary and Joseph, until the time was come for him to go out and begin his more open work in the waiting world.

"After Nazareth," said Will, "the place where Christ dwelt oftenest was Capernaum, on the shore of the Lake of Gennesaret. We must rest now to be ready for an early start to-morrow, and a ride as far as the lake, through Cana to Tiberias."

CHAPTER XXII.

NAZARETH TO TIBERIAS.

"Elias, it is nearly seven o'clock. See if the horses are ready."

"They are at the door, sir."

"Then we will start. Good-by, Fra Johannes. We are glad to have found so worthy a host to entertain pilgrims here in the home of our Lord. You might easily have done much towards making our recollection of Nazareth the opposite of what it will now always be. If all travellers remember you as we shall, you must have a wide circle of friends. Good-by."

"Good-by, sir."

They rode through the town, past the fountain, where the water-carriers were still busier than they had been the evening before, and up the hills opposite those they had descended in entering the town. Looking back they were impressed again with the beauty of the scene before them, where the town, with its stone churches and convents, lay among its fifteen rounded hills "like the centre of a flower among its petals," Harry suggested.

They crossed the ridge, and the picture was shut away from their sight. A ride to the northeast of about four and a half miles brought them to "Kefr Kenna," a miserable village with a few stone and mortar houses and forlorn-looking inhabitants. It is Cana of Galilee,* where the Saviour attended the wedding-feast and made water wine,† where the nobleman of Capernaum came to ask Jesus to go down and heal his son,‡ and where the apostle Nathanael was born.§

As they entered the narrow lanes between the houses they were at once besieged by a troop of boys, eager to hold their horses while they visited the room reputed to be that in which the first miracle was performed. In their eagerness, and their hope of obtaining backsheesh, these boys were altogether too forward; they were troublesome.

Harry had been a little way behind. Now he rode up beside his cousin. "Cousin Will," he said, "do you know, I feel as though I had just done a wicked thing—those fellows were so troublesome! They wanted to lead my horse. I told them to clear out; but one of them, a tall,

---

* There is a rival site farther north in "Kana el Jelîl." Its name is strongly in its favor, while tradition is on the side of Kefr Kenna.   † John 2:1-11.   ‡ John 4:46-50.   § John 21:2.

slim fellow, laid his hand on my bridle. I had not seen his face at all; I only noticed that he seemed to be rather the leader among them. I hardly thought what I was doing, but I just drew my whip, lightly enough, across his hand. It wasn't a hard blow, but he let go and turned towards me, just surprised, not angry, apparently, in the least. It seemed as though I had struck the child Jesus! For there was that very same type of face looking up at me which, you remember, we saw once before in Damascus—which you called a typical face and said was like that which many of the old painters used in making their pictures of Christ. It really startled me! There is the boy now. I wish you'd call him up and let him hold all the horses. And I'll give him double backsheesh besides."

"You are right," said Will. "It is that same peculiar type: jet-black hair, an intense face, dark and sensitive, with black eyes, the whole form slight and graceful. It is strange that we should have found it just here."

They were taken into the feast-room.

"This is not suggestive of weddings and merriment," said Will; "it is too dark and dingy. The place seems to be a sort of chapel now, with its altar, and lamp burning before the shrine."

"I wonder," said Harry, "if the people suppose that those six earthen jars along the wall are the original stone ones?"

"Very likely. But we have seen all there is here, and different enough everything is, house and all, from what we imagine the place to have been where the wedding-feast was held and the first recorded miracle of the Lord was performed."

Towards the middle of the afternoon they were riding along an extended plateau—though without appreciating how high they were above the sea, the ascent had been so gradual and irregular.

"Would you like, sir, to ride over to that hill for the sake of the view from it?" asked Elias, pointing to a rocky ridge of ground, some sixty feet high in the highest part, a quarter of a mile away on the left.

"Is it especially interesting there?"

"It is a very good view, sir."

"What hill is it? I supposed there was no view about here at all equal to Mount Tabor."

Elias gave some name, but one they were not familiar with.

"Is there any path to it?"

"No, sir; but we can find our way across the country."

"I think it's not worth while, Harry, taking

the time. I am in a hurry to reach Tiberias and the Sea of Galilee."

"So am I."

But after a few minutes Will spoke again:

"Yet we are hardly wise. There is time enough to reach Tiberias easily before dark, and if we fail to climb this hill we may be losing more than we think. Elias, lead the way there by the smoothest path you can find."

But the smoothest way was too rough for fast riding. They could only walk their horses over stony, uneven ground. Crossing the comparatively level space in front they neared the foot of the hill. There were two slight elevations of unequal height connected by an irregular central ridge.

They rode leisurely up the gradual ascent. Several times they stopped while Harry dismounted to gather new varieties of flowers that were abundant all about them. There was one variety especially that attracted them, a bright, star-shaped flower of crimson and black—anemones the natives call them, according to Elias.

Said Harry, "If we can press these so that they will keep their colors till we reach home, I believe they will be the prettiest flowers that we have found. Cousin Will, I wonder what we shall see in just a few minutes more? I imagine not very much; the hill isn't high enough; but I'm curious to know. I'll ride ahead and look."

As he reached the top of the ridge Will saw him stop suddenly and heard him cry out in astonishment. He had good reason to do so. Will in turn urged his horse forward up to Harry's side. There he sat for a while without a word. Then he dismounted and, signing to Elias to stay behind with the horses, walked off to the farthest point of the ridge. By nothing that he had ever seen before had he been impressed as he was by this. He wanted to be alone. Presently he beckoned to Harry, who had also dismounted, to join him.

"Harry, it is not too much to say this has been just overwhelming to me! I have felt more nearly than I ever have before, and more, I imagine, than I shall at Jerusalem itself, what the old Crusaders felt at their first sight of the Holy City: they were ready to throw themselves from their horses and kneel down on the ground and cover their faces. The unexpectedness of it all adds to the effect of it. I know well enough now where we are. We are on Mount Hattîn. These are the 'Horns of Hattîn.' It is the place where Christ spoke to the disciples the Sermon on the Mount, the Mount of the Beatitudes. It is the

New Testament Mount Sinai.* Because we approached from the west we thought it was only a little hill, sixty feet high or so; but here on this side it goes sheer down five hundred feet, steep almost as a precipice, to the plain, which appears from this distance smooth as a floor; and then down again five hundred feet more to the blue gem there, dark as the bluest sky—a sapphire set in the midst of circle after circle of receding hills and mountains, with Mount Hermon as the last, snow-crowned in the north; that gem which is the gem of the whole world, the Sea of Galilee.

> O shining sea! O silver-sweet
>   Æolian harp of Galilee,
> No wind-swept waves in all the world
>   Can speak like thee.
>
> The softest ripples on thy shore,
>   Thy wildest waves, cannot forget;
> World-words of love, world-words of peace,
>   They echo yet.
>
> O gem, set deep among the hills
>   Of Galilee! O sacred sea,
> Once swept by Jesus' breath in words
>   That deathless be,
>
> Upon this mount where Jesus taught,
>   This altar reared in lofty state,
> I yield myself anew to Him
>   Who made thee great.

---

* The site of the Sermon on the Mount is not fully determined, but tradition and fitness point to Mount Hattin.

They delayed as long as it was possible for them to delay, if they were to reach Tiberias before dark. Then they mounted and turned reluctantly away. When they had descended the Horns they kept to the right so as to reach the village of Hattîn at the foot of the mountain.

As they rode Will said, "It was 1,800 years ago, Harry, when that first multitude was gathered here, according to tradition, to listen to the Saviour saying, with the other beatitudes, 'Blessed are the peacemakers.' History tells that nearly 1,200 years later a very different multitude met, not to seek peace, but to fight in one of the deadliest conflicts of the Crusades.

"It was in the year 1187. A truce had been agreed upon between the Saracens and the Crusaders; but the latter had violated it. A band of them, under the command of Raynald of Châtillon, had plundered a rich caravan on its way from Damascus to Arabia. When restitution could not be obtained, Sultan Saladin marched with a great army into Palestine. He met the Crusaders on this plain of Hattîn—2,000 knights, 8,000 heavy-armed foot-soldiers, and many light troops beside.

"The battle began at daybreak; and at once what is always terrible became exceptionally so.

On both sides the fight was for religion; on both it was for dominion. On the side of the Crusaders it soon became also a battle for life. They were out-generaled at every point; they were surrounded. They failed even to obtain water, though close by, near the village of Hattîn, there was a fountain of the best of water; and soon they were perishing from thirst under the intense heat of the July sun.

"They became desperate. The Holy Cross, which the bishops of Acre and Lydda had brought to the war from Jerusalem, was already captured. Many of the bravest were slain. There was no hope. The battle became a slaughter. A small company of knights, those of Count Raymond, drew together, and charged through the enemy's ranks and escaped towards Tyre. The others, the few who were left alive, were pressed back to the Horns. There they fought a little longer. Three times the Saracens charged up the slope, and then the fight was ended. Some had been forced over the edge of the precipice. The rest, with the King of Jerusalem among them, surrendered. Saladin received the captives in his tent. Most of them he received with kindness; but the one man whose violation of the truce had renewed the war he cut down before them all with his own sword. Afterwards two hundred knights were beheaded. The king and the princes were imprisoned in Damascus.

"It was the death-blow to the power of the Crusaders in Palestine. By September most of the lesser strongholds of the country were occupied, and in October Jerusalem itself yielded to Saladin."

After a steep descent from the upper plain the travellers regained a beaten path near the village of Hattîn. They entered the village, and, finding their way among the flat-roofed, irregularly-placed huts, came out beyond on the lower plain, or, rather, plateau, which they had looked down upon from the Horns of Hattîn, that towered now above them five hundred feet against the sky.

Their course lay across this plateau by an easy path towards the lake, which was now hidden again in its deep basin.

"You can't see Tiberias or the lake, sir," said Elias, "until we are close upon them. The descent to them is very steep. But we are nearly there."

Soon they reached the abrupt edge of the plateau. They were close above the lake; and the town of Tiberias, with its ruined walls and poor houses, lay immediately below them.

They accomplished safely the steep descent—

it was the second of the two steps down from the summit of Mount Hattîn—and entered the town by what was once a gateway, but now seemed hardly more than a break in the ruined wall.

Within, not far from the gate, they found the Latin hospice. It furnished them with fairly comfortable quarters; though neither in its accommodations nor in its brethren did it equal the hospice at Nazareth, excepting that here, back of the house, was a pleasant little garden, walled in, and carefully kept in simple style by one of the monks.

As soon as possible Will and Harry sallied from the hospice. Outside the heavy gate of the courtyard a lane led down to the left, along which women and children were passing, carrying large earthen water-jars balanced on their heads and shoulders; and men too were there, leading their horses and donkeys and goats to drink. Following this lane they came to the lake—came to a silvery beach sloping evenly down to the rippling waters of what seemed to them, as they stooped and touched it, the sacred Sea of Galilee.

Close by was a ruined tower of black stone. They clambered to it. There they could see the fair lake stretching away far to the north and south. Behind them were old fortifications of the

Crusaders, and opposite, the gray cliffs of the eastern shore.

Presently they returned. Then they wandered for a time through the intricate, dirty streets of the once beautiful town—this namesake of the great Emperor Tiberius. As the sun was setting they came again to the edge of the lake for one more look at its beauty. And there they gained for themselves a bright "good night" before returning to the gloomy hospice; for drifting slowly by the spot where they stood went a clumsy sail-boat filled full with a merry crowd of young people with bright faces, in holiday dress. They were singing, and as they sang they accompanied their voices loudly with a rhythmic clapping of their hands. Catching sight of Will and Harry the singers signaled to them with their hands and voices, and when the signal was returned redoubled their music and laughter and noise.

"If we could translate their singing," said Will, "the jingle would be something like this:

> Thus we row, lightly now,
>   On the sea;
> Singing free, glad as thou,
>   Galilee.
>
> Like thy waves beating time
>   On our boat,
> Beat our hands to our rhyme
>   While we float.

> Shadows deep round us creep,
>   Now good night;
> Spirits kind watch will keep
>   Till the light. Good night.

So singing and laughing they drifted out of sight. And when the travellers had seen the moon shining above the lake they too drifted away into the land of dreams.

CHAPTER XXIII.

THE SHORE OF GENNESARET.

"WHAT was it Elias was so excited about just now, Cousin Will?"

"When I asked where the horses were, he said that Hassan told him we were going to Tell Hûm to-day by boat, and that travellers never made the trip with horses."

"Did n't he know better than that?"

"Certainly he did, but he hoped we did not. He wanted a holiday for himself and Hassan. It would be nonsense to take a boat to-day. It would be pleasant if we could be sure of the wind and could stop as we shall want to along the way; but the water now is like glass, and it is likely to stay so. It would be dangerously hot too on the water. It promises to be the hottest day we have had yet."

"What did you tell Elias?"

"To say to Hassan that we would be ready to mount in exactly fifteen minutes."

In fifteen minutes they mounted at the hospice gate. Their day's ride was to be northward along the lake as far as Tell Hûm, and back to

TIBERIAS AND THE SEA OF GALILEE.

Tiberias for another night. This would take them to four places of interest, the "Round Fountain" and "Fountain of the Fig-tree" on the Plain of Gennesaret, Tabighah just beyond, and north of that again Tell Hûm, one of which places marks the location of ancient Capernaum, but which one is undetermined.

As they left Tiberias their course led at first, by a narrow path, along the face of hills that advance to the very edge of the water. Here the view includes nearly the whole lake.

"How large is this Sea of Galilee?" asked Harry.

"About thirteen miles long and five miles across here; seven miles at the widest part. Tiberias lies some five miles from the southern end of the lake, and is the only town of any importance on the whole shore."*

They were at the narrowest and worst part of the cliff path when they saw a loaded camel approaching. They made haste to give as much room as possible. That at the best would have been no more than enough; but while the others passed safely, Will's horse balked when he tried

---

* Tiberias was built in the time of Christ, by Herod Antipas, who named it in honor of the Emperor Tiberius, and made it his capital. It is mentioned but three times in the Bible, and no visit of Christ to it is recorded.

to force him to the edge of the path. No wonder, for it looked like a choice for the horse between a fall over the rocks for himself or a fall from his back for his rider. Before Will could master him, the camel was swinging down close upon them, swaying heavily like a ship in rough water, a foot or so to each side as he came.

As he passed the swing was towards Will. In an instant they struck sharply, and horse and camel and man were struggling together. It was a collision, not between ships at sea or of knights in harness, but between a horse with its rider and a camel, and with the advantage wholly on the camel's side.

It was quickly over. They had crowded past, and Will had kept his seat; but he had no inclination to challenge another joust.

"I came out better than I hoped," he said. "I wonder what the camel's load was. Certainly it was not bags of grain. It felt against my knee like stone."

The path improved.

"Cousin Will, do you believe in witches flying through the air?" asked Harry; "because, if you do, I think a flock of them must have got snarled up in that tree, and escaped only with the loss of a good part of their clothes;" and he pointed to a solitary tree ten or fifteen feet high.

"It does look strange," said Will. "Shreds of cloth of all colors and materials are fluttering from every part of it. Elias, what does all that mean?"

"It is a sacred tree, sir, and the bits of clothes are the offerings of pilgrims, mostly of those going for their health to the warm baths south of Tiberias."

"A flowering bush of that species would make a sensation at home," remarked Harry. "I wonder if I can't pick one of the blossoms."

"I would n't try. You had better be satisfied with these crowds of oleanders; or here is a pretty bush and a new one, with pink, funnel-shaped flowers. They are like little morning-glories that are tired of climbing and so have decided to blossom on a bush instead of a vine."

"Well, I will take one of them for the press and put it next to the 'anemone' that we have to remind us of Mount Hattîn."

But Harry had a pleasanter reminder still to bring away. They saw a poor native coming along the path towards them. He was carrying a load of wood, and had besides in his hand a bunch of some delicately scented green herb. As he passed the travellers and they were anticipating a demand for backsheesh, or an indifferent or hostile stare, instead he quietly slipped the plant he held into Harry's hand, and with a kindly look kept on his way.

"Indeed that pleases me," said Will. "It was a small matter, but it was genuine kindness, doing a pleasant thing for entire strangers with no thought of reward."

"I don't know what it is," said Harry, "that he has given me, but it shall certainly have a place of honor among my flowers."

About three miles north of Tiberias the hills drew back, at the most two miles, from the shore, and made room at their feet for the lovely Plain of Gennesaret, about three miles long. The place was covered now with flowers and grass on its pasture land, and with great fields of grain divided only by bushy water-courses, and along the shore where their path wound with clumps of flaming oleanders.

As they descended to the plain, Magdala lay at their left, a miserable village now of a few stone and clay huts, but once the home of one of the faithful Marys of the New Testament story— Mary Magdalene.

Near Magdala they came to a large Arab encampment. The tents were pitched, and about them were feeding cattle and unloaded camels.

"Harry, I expect we shall have no better chance than this for an experiment you ought to try somewhere in Palestine. You have been riding horses and donkeys; do n't you want to try a camel? We have seen plenty of the awkward beasts, but you can't appreciate them until you've been on one."

"It's just what I want to do! And big as they are, if I do n't keep on better than I did on that bit of a donkey at Gibraltar I'll feel as though I ought to go to riding sheep."

The old fellow they finally hired looked as if he had been through the wars, with patches of matted hair over his body, and a big beard, and callous pads at his knees. Harry at once dubbed him "Methuselah."

"Methuselah, you need grooming. Would I like to do it? No, sir, not while you are showing your teeth in that style, and craning your long neck round and hissing like a great cat. So you do n't want to mind your master and get down on your knees for me! Have you the rheumatism? I'd think so by the fuss you make. There, now you're down! Mr. Arab, you can't understand my language, I know; but I make signs to you. Please to just keep between him and my skin until I'm on top of him. If he's to nip either of us, I must say I'd rather it would be you. Am I ready? No. Keep him down till I get a good hold in front."

Will laughed.

"What are you laughing at, Cousin Will?"

"You'll know in a minute."

"Now I'm ready; up with you, old fellow." And leaning well forward, Harry pulled at his head.

But he had forgotten—with camels it is the other end that gets up first. It was sudden, very; he found himself more nearly astride the camel's neck than his back; but before he got his breath he was pitched the other way, for now it was the front end that was getting up.

However, he kept on top somewhere, and now settled himself again in the saddle. He laughed down at Will.

"Why did n't you tell me that they get up cow-fashion instead of horse-fashion? You knew a roll on the grass would n't hurt me? Well, I was near taking it. Now go ahead, Methuselah. Ah, I have no more faith in your rheumatism!" And he shouted back to Will, "I'm glad I got used to rough weather on the 'Norman Monarch;' you'd think there was a big sea running if you were up here."

And so he disappeared beyond the high oleander-bushes, with the Arab running before. He soon returned, and brought his steed to a halt at Will's side and slid to the ground.

"It's a good sort of gymnastics, Cousin Will. It doesn't take long that way to get all the shaking one wants. Alexander the Great on Bucephalus isn't to be compared to it."

They remounted their horses and rode away. A little to the west of the encampment was the deep ravine down which they might have come the day before, from Mount Hattin, if they had not preferred the other route across the plateau to Tiberias.

"Cousin Will, that's a wild-looking place."

"Yes, and there has been wild work there. Do you see those dark spots high up on the face of the precipice?"

"Yes."

"They are entrances to caverns which honeycomb the whole rock. With the village above them they used to be called Arbela. In the time of Herod the Great they were an almost impregnable stronghold for robbers. Josephus tells how difficult it was for the king's army, which had marched against them, to dislodge them.* The precipice was so steep and high it was impossible to climb to the caverns. What could the soldiers do? At last they tried making large chests, which were filled with armed men, and then lowered by means of iron chains to the mouth of

* "Antiquities," Book XIV. Ch. XV.

the caves. Then when the robbers rushed out against them the soldiers caught them with long hooks, and pulling them off, dashed them down the precipice to the rocks below. Or where they kept out of reach and under cover the soldiers would leave the chests and either charge into the caves or build fires at their mouths to fill them with smoke, and so suffocate or burn to death the wretched victims.

"Some surrendered; some preferred to die. In one cave there was an old man, with his wife and seven sons—for the robbers had their families with them, and their property. The others were ready to yield; but the father would not assent, though the soldiers, and Herod himself, offered them pardon. He would rather that all should die. One after the other he slew his sons and the mother, and cast their bodies down the precipice. Then he cast himself after them.

"By such methods the difficult work yonder along the face of those cliffs was accomplished. The robbers were exterminated."

They were riding now across the plain in search of the "Round Fountain." Elias did not know where it was. He had never visited it. He had inquired at Magdala, and thought he could find it; but, as it was, they only happened upon it. They were already a mile and a half from the lake-shore when, off to the right of their course, Will spied, among thick bushes, what looked to him like a circular pile of low masonry. He pointed it out to Elias.

"That cannot be the place, sir."

"I think it is. At any rate I am going to see."

He dismounted and pushed his way through the brush.

"This is it. Come on, Harry," he called back.

And Harry followed.

The fountain proved to be a shallow pool of clear water, over fifty feet in diameter, and surrounded with a solid wall of hewn stones.

"Why does any one think that Capernaum was here?" asked Harry.

"We know from the Bible that the city was on or near this plain,* and not far from the seashore.† And Josephus says‡ that the plain is watered by a highly fertilizing spring called Capharnaum by the natives. And he adds, as if he considered it a thing easily possible, that some have supposed the fountain to be connected underground with the river Nile because it produces a fish similar to the Coracin of Egypt. All that

---

* Compare John 6 : 17 with Matt. 14 : 34 and Mark 6 : 53.
† Matt. 4 : 13; 9 : 1; 13 : 1; Mark 2 : 13; John 6 : 17.
‡ "Wars." Book III. ch. X.

would seem to imply that the fountain he was describing lay at a considerable distance from the lake."

"There are fish enough in here now," said Harry, "and how tame they are! But I see no ruins about."

"There are arguments for and against each of the different sites, and as yet there is no conclusive proof for either of them, and I doubt if there ever will be. Now we will hasten on to the 'Fountain of the Fig-tree' at the northern end of the plain. The way would be shortened if we could ride directly towards it, but there is no getting the horses through the tangles of bushes and vines on the banks of this stream. It is of no use for you to try, Elias. We will ride back to the lake and then keep the path along the shore."

In about an hour the hills closed in again abruptly before them, ending the plain and shutting it in completely from whatever was beyond. There was no room for a goat even to pass between the cliff and the water.

Only a few feet back from the lake and at the very foot of the precipice grows a gnarled, ragged, rock-grasping fig-tree. Its roots are coiled like snakes over and among the boulders. Either from this rugged patriarch among fig-trees, or from some member of its long line of ancestors, the fountain beneath takes its name. It is called "Ain et Tîn," the Fountain of the Fig-tree.

It is a romantic place, and a favorite camping-ground for travellers and shepherds. There is no village near it now. There is only a ruinous khan, Khan Minyeh, by which name the place is sometimes called, and which Dr. Robinson and many others regard as the site of ancient Capernaum.

The travellers rested for a while in the shade of the fig-tree and refreshed themselves from the fountain. Then they betook themselves to the path leading over the cliffs towards Tabighah.* As they climbed, Will said,

"This reminds me of the 'Ladder of Tyre,' only all here is on a much smaller scale. But do you notice a curious thing about this path? It is hewn in the solid rock like a long trough or aqueduct, and an even grade seems to have been carefully kept all the way. Some believe that once the abundant waters at Tabighah were carried in this trough across the hill, to be used in irrigating the northern part of the Plain of Gennesaret and for supplying the city there (which possibly was Capernaum) with more water than the Fountain of the Fig-tree could give. The fountains of Tabighah are lower than this ridge, but they are so powerful the water could easily have been raised

* Tabighah is fifteen minutes from Ain et Tîn.

to the required level. You can see Tabighah now below us."

"Yes; and it must once have been quite a place, with all those ruined walls and aqueducts and arches. And what a fine rush of water there is all about. It is not one stream that we have to ford, but many little streams, coming from all directions. This is fine. I would like a bath here."

"We had better wait and take that in the lake at Tell Hûm."

"This, you said, is another of the sites claimed for Capernaum."

"Yes, some make that claim; and others think the place was a large manufacturing suburb of Capernaum. Now thirty minutes farther north, and we will reach the limit of our ride at Tell Hûm."

Thirty minutes over rolling hills, and they were at Tell Hûm.

"Oh, what a desolate place this is!" exclaimed Harry; "hot, no fountains, scarcely a tree, no living thing in sight, excepting that one dog barking at us; no houses, excepting those few miserable huts; no ruins either that are anything but loose piles of black stones!"

"If this was Capernaum, the woe that Christ pronounced against it has surely come to pass.[*]

[*] Matt. 11:23.

You notice, Harry, there are more signs here of a large city than we have found elsewhere—unless at Tabighah. From the top of this stone hut you can see that a large part of the slope of the hill is covered with ruins, such as they are, all overgrown with weeds and briers."

"And they are all of black stone."

"Most of them are—of black basalt. But do you see over there those white stones lying together? Not many; only a few. They are of pure, pink-veined marble, and some of them are very finely carved. Possibly they are parts of what was once a small and beautiful synagogue of the Jews; perhaps it was the synagogue which the centurion built whose servant Christ healed in Capernaum."*

"Do you suppose these huts are occupied now?"

"Not permanently; only by wandering shepherds."

"How many lizards there are running over the stones! They seem to enjoy the fiercely hot sun."

"Now suppose we take our bath, while Elias arranges lunch in the shadow of this wall. Elias, we will be back in a few minutes."

* Luke 7:5. So careful an authority as Lieut. Warren says, "If Tell Hûm be Capernaum, this is without doubt the synagogue built by the Roman centurion."

"It's a poor place to eat in, sir."

"Why so?"

"Can't we go back to Ain et Tîn?"

"That will take too long. I'm hungry."

"There's no water here, sir."

"But you can bring it from the lake."

"I can't stop here, sir. I'm afraid."

"You are afraid! Of what?"

"Of snakes, sir—terribly afraid of them. If I saw one, I'd run from here to Jerusalem. And this is just the place for them, sir."

"Well, well; you are a brave fellow! I should think you would be ashamed of yourself."

"I am; but I can't help it, sir."

"Evidently you cannot; so just spread a bit of something to eat on this flat rock, keeping a good look-out all the while for your foes; then get on your horse and sit there, out of their reach, till we have bathed and eaten. We will not be long. Then we will ride back and finish our lunch and our nooning under the arches at Tabighah."

The shore here was stony; but they enjoyed their bath notwithstanding. Returning, they took a bite of food, then mounted and rode back to Tabighah.

There, under an arch of old masonry that shielded them from the hot sun, by the side of swift streams, they finished their lunch and rested for an hour.

Since starting, here and there along the shore Harry had picked up pretty little shells and pocketed them. He spread them out now on the rock where they were sitting.

Said Will, "I would keep some of the nicest of those, Harry. You could arrange them prettily at home, perhaps in the shape of a cross or an anchor; and then you could write under them words something like these:

>Shells that were born where the sacred sea
>Mirrors the hills of Galilee,
>Softly your pearly lips whisper to me
>Words that are sweet as words can be;
>Only the words that the Master gave,
>Stilling Gennesaret's raging wave,
>But words that were signs of his mighty will—
>You whisper them yet, his 'Peace, be still.'

"Isn't that pretty! Indeed, I'll keep the shells. They will please Nellie and Mary."

When they were ready to start again, after their noon rest, the horses had wandered off across the water, and Elias was nowhere to be seen. They sent a small Arab, who had been an attentive spectator as they ate, in search of him. Presently he returned with a bigger Arab, who offered to carry them on his back over the stream. That was easier than to try to ford it. He landed them safely on the southern bank. Elias and the horses were found. They crossed the ridge again, delayed for a few minutes at the Fountain of the Fig-tree, skirted the shore of the Plain of Gennesaret, and reached Magdala.

All day the heat had been intense. The sea-basin, lying as it does six hundred feet below the level of the Mediterranean, and having all its coasts shut in by hills, at times is like an oven. It was so to-day. And there had been no breath of wind to temper the heat. The water had been like glass, and it was like glass as they rode past Magdala. But in five minutes more a great surge of wind, from the gorges to the west, had rushed down upon them, and sweeping across the sea was beating its waters white. In ten or fifteen minutes a gale was blowing, from the force of which they were glad to be somewhat sheltered as they passed within the line of cliffs towards Tiberias.

"These sudden storms are peculiar to the lake," said Will; "I am glad we are experiencing one of them. It must have been like this that night when Christ saved his disciples from shipwreck, when he rebuked the winds and the sea, and they obeyed him, and there was a great calm."*

* Matt. 8: 26.

MOUNT TABOR.

CHAPTER XXIV.

MOUNT TABOR.

"WE have a picturesque addition to our caravan this morning," said Harry, as they took the path from Tiberias towards Mount Tabor.

"Yes, Elias was telling me about it: a little white donkey and its tall Mohammedan master. They belong in Jerusalem. They are on their way back after a pilgrimage for the man's health to the hot baths below Tiberias."

"What a queer pair it is! You would think the man could carry the donkey as well as the donkey could the man. His feet nearly touch the ground as he rides. If they prove as interesting as they are odd-looking, we shall be glad of their company."

The time from Tiberias to Mount Tabor is about five and a half hours. The route is past Khan el Tujjar (Khan of the merchants) towards the southwest.

They came at last in sight of the mountain. "Tabor is finer than I supposed," said Harry. "I knew its shape was something like a haystack, but I had no idea the haystack was as large as it is."

"The summit is more than a thousand feet above the Plain of Esdraelon, and nearly two thousand above the Mediterranean. It and Mount Carmel are the finest mountains in this region, as well as among the most interesting ones historically. You remember that when we crossed the Kishon we talked about the gathering here of the Israelites under Barak and Deborah, before they marched down to attack Sisera.* That is the chief event of all that are recorded as having ever happened on Tabor. As to the shape of the mountain, it varies according to the side one views it from. From the north and south its outline is nearly the arc of a circle, as we see it now; but from the east it is a truncated cone with the summit slightly rounded, while from the west it is wedge-shaped. All this side is covered with a forest of oak-trees and terebinth and mock-orange; but on the other side there is little besides bare limestone cliffs. See how fine the trees are in front of us! They cover the mountain to the very top. The oaks are equal to those we passed on our way to Nazareth."

"We ought to lunch under one of them again," said Harry.

"We will; and it is near enough noon to camp now."

* Judges 4:6–15.

After lunch they undertook the steeper part of the ascent. There is but one path that can be followed on horseback, and even that in places is scarcely safe. Once especially Will's horse was nearly down. The little white donkey did the best. It seemed as sure-footed and unconcerned over the rough paths as a goat. They reached the summit without serious accident. There they rode through extensive ruins to the hospice where they were to spend the night.

"Why! judging from the amount of tumble-down walls all about," exclaimed Harry; "there must once have been a good many people living up here."

"There were," said Will. "The Old Testament references render it probable that either a town or a fortress, or perhaps both, existed here as early as the time of Joshua; and we know from Josephus that a fortified city was here sixty years after Christ. In the time of the Crusaders churches and convents were erected by them. So these ruins mark a long and very varied history. No one lives here now excepting the few monks who have charge of the hospice, with their attendants. The nearest village is at the foot of the mountain."

After supper they climbed to the roof of the hospice by the rough steps and ladders, and waited there while the sun went down grandly over what is perhaps the most varied and suggestive view that any single mountain-top of equal height in Palestine or in the world can give. Far-away snow-capped Hermon bounded the view in the north; Gilboa and the hills of Samaria were in the south; the valley of the Jordan was to the east; the Mediterranean Sea far off in the west. The great Plain of Esdraelon which they had crossed, and the heights around it, had been the scene of great battles and wonderful miracles, the memory of which was recalled by the names of Joshua and Gideon, of Ahab, Elijah, and Elisha, of Saul and Jonathan, of our Lord himself, and of Napoleon and Kleber in modern times. For a while they talked over the events of deep interest which this view brought to mind; then they clambered to the ground and went within doors out of the cold, for the nights are cold there, up towards the stars, almost two thousand feet above the sea.

CHAPTER XXV.

MOUNT TABOR TO JEZREEL.

"Come Harry, it's morning again. Don't you hear the pigs grunting about the door? and somebody is thrashing one of the dogs till he yelps again. The chapel bell is ringing. Horses and oxen and roosters and dogs and pigs and men are all evidently awake."

"I should think they were," sleepily growled Harry, as he tumbled out of bed. "If only the donkey would join in now!"

The morning was clear and bracing. While waiting for breakfast they wandered away from the noise and uncleanness of the hospice inclosure to the ruins near by of the "Crusaders' Church," and through a break in the surrounding wall looked off again over the beautiful view across the Sea of Galilee to the now familiar northern landmark of snowy Hermon.

After breakfast they were not sorry to leave the hospice. Their impression was that a not very saintly community was located in the ancient and sacred place.

"We shall make better progress down the

mountain on foot than on horseback," said Will. "I suppose, Elias, the path is the same that we came up by."

"Yes, sir, and you can save a good distance by cutting off the curves in the steepest places."

Will and Harry walked ahead, and were soon far down the mountain. Finally they stopped on a large rock under an oak to wait for the horses. And they waited and waited.

"It seems to me they are a long while getting down," remarked Will at last.

"Look there, Cousin Will; isn't that the white donkey away off there to the right, bobbing along like a big sheep?"

"Yes, and there is Elias on the rocks still farther away, and Hassan and the horses are nowhere in sight."

"Do you see! the donkey's master is beckoning to us! We must be on the wrong path."

"Then they misdirected us. They said there was no turn. But you remember we noticed a path just above here crossing this at right angles. No doubt they turned there."

"It's well we stopped to rest when we did."

"And well the white donkey was there to catch your eye."

In a few minutes they caught up with the horses, and, mounting, rode slowly towards the south. But they were not clear of the mountain yet. They came out upon bold bluffs overhanging the southern plain.

"Here we can see," said Will, "as though it was a great map spread before us, almost the whole of our route for to-day. Right below us is Debûrieh, so called, possibly, after the prophetess Deborah. At any rate the two names are the same. From the village you can see our path leading across the plain towards Endor on the heights opposite, where the witch lived, to see whom Saul risked so much on the night before his fatal battle with the Philistines.*

"Not far off to the right, on the same spur of hills, lies Nain. You remember how the Saviour met there the funeral procession bearing from the city the dead body of the widow's only son, whom He raised to life and restored to his mother.†

"Then around the hill we will come to Sûlem, the ancient Shunem,‡ the town of the 'Shunammite woman' who built a little chamber on the wall of her house and furnished it with 'a bed and a table, and a stool and a candlestick' for the prophet Elisha,§ and who was herself most highly favored by the 'holy man of God;' it is the place, too, where the Philistines were encamped

---

* 1 Sam. 28:7 ff. † Luke 7:11 ff.
‡ Present Arabic name, Solam. § 2 Kings 4:10.

the night that Saul went to Endor.* And opposite Shunem at Jezreel, that same night, the Israelites were stationed ready for battle. On the plain between, the battle was to be fought. From Jezreel there will be a long ride across the Plain of Esdraelon to Jenîn. There the plain meets the hills of Samaria, and there we will spend the night, if the town can furnish any sort of a fit lodging-place.

"Now we will move on and find what all these places prove to be upon nearer acquaintance, and what our reception will be in them. Endor has no very desirable reputation. You know some one was telling us before we left Beirût of trouble he once had there. And there is a chance too of our meeting Bedouins on the plain."

It was a scramble again safely made (but only by dismounting and taking it on foot) down to the base of the mountain. Then there was an easy path, with a chance at last for a gallop across the plain, which is an offshoot of the Plain of Esdraelon, towards Endor.

"How unusually attractive the village looks," said Will, as they drew near to Endor clinging to the steep slope of the hills among its trees. "But what a hubbub there is among the people."

* 1 Sam. 28:4.

"I hope it is n't anything about us that causes it," said Harry.

"It looks more like a quarrel among themselves."

Elias undertook to guide them up into the village, and to the "Witches' Cave" above it, but he lost his way at the very first. They were between two rows of huts, and the lane in front was too steep to climb.

"Harry," said Will, "do n't you want some exercise? Suppose you dismount and walk up."

"Indeed I'll not! and I do n't believe you would advise it. I do n't care to be eaten alive. I should think there were more half-starved, ugly curs here than there are men. There comes another one, full tilt at the horses' heels, and he's starting out all his friends and neighbors! Whew! what a yelping. It's worse than Constantinople and Damascus. I suppose if I were to jump down among them they would run, but I would n't care to try it unless there was need."

"Elias, if you do n't know the way, say so, and ask some of these men to guide us."

By inquiring they at last found the Witches' Cave. It is in the face of the hill above the village. They dismounted and went inside through the narrow entrance. Two old hags were there, homely and wild-looking enough, one of them especially, to have served as models for the original witch, if, indeed, she was anything like what most imagine her to have been. With a sort of pail made of leather they were dipping up water for the horses from a spring that half filled the cavern.

Quite a company had gathered by the time Will and Harry were ready to remount. They gave liberal fees to the women who had watered the horses, and to three or four men and boys besides, who had served as guides and hitching-posts, and rode off towards Nain, leaving the whole party in high good humor.

"I think," said Harry, "the people of Endor have been slandered. Their chief fault is that they keep too many villanous curs."

Nain, three-quarters of an hour away, is of interest only as associated with the raising from the dead the widow's son. Now it is nothing but a small, dilapidated village.

Beyond Nain the path curved around the hill until Shunem was in sight, lying a little below them among its orchards and long hedges of cactus.

"They have here a new style of fencing," remarked Harry, as they rode through the town.

"Yes, and a very efficient kind it is. It would not be possible to get through these prickly cactus-hedges without cutting one's way; and they make an attractive show besides, with their yellow blossoms."

They lunched in a grove of fig-trees. It was inclosed by a high cactus-hedge, which in one place had been partly broken down, leaving an arched passage-way, under which they rode. The horses and the white donkey were turned loose among the trees. The rugs were spread in a shady place for Will and Harry. At a little distance Elias and Hassan and the white donkey's master made their coffee and smoked and gossiped.

In the afternoon the ride was first across the plain lying in front of Shunem, and the scene of Saul's battle with the Philistines,* to Jezreel.

"Think how different a place this must have been in King Ahab's time," said Will, as they climbed the steep ascent of a hundred feet to the town. "It was the favorite city of Ahab, where he and his wicked queen, Jezebel, held their court. But after Jehu seized the government and destroyed the house of Ahab the place lost its importance. We can look out now over the plain, just as the watchman and the queen and Joram were doing on that last day. They saw some one driving furiously down there to the

* 1 Sam. 31:1.

east, whose driving, they said, was like the driving of Jehu. King Joram went out to meet him, and Jehu drew a bow with his full strength and slew him in his chariot. There are no walls and high windows now in Jezreel, but there were then. As Jehu entered the city the painted queen looked from one of the windows above the gateway. He called to those with her to cast her out; and she was thrown under the horses' feet and trodden to death. So Jehu reigned, and prophecy was fulfilled; and the glory of Jezreel began to fade to what we see about us now."*

Will referred once more, as they left the village, to Saul's fate.

"Do you see those higher hills to the southeast," he asked, "of which this is a spur?"

"Yes."

"They are the 'hills of Gilboa.'"

"Where Saul died?"

"Where Saul and Jonathan died, and many another with them. Saul fled there after the stray arrow had pierced his armor in the battle with the Philistines. He was defeated and wounded. He could not escape. When his armor-bearer refused to slay him, he drew his own sword and fell upon it and died.†

"All the nation mourned for the great ones

* 2 Kings 9.   † 1 Sam. 31 : 3-6.

who had fallen. David especially lamented, with unequalled tenderness, over the beauty of Israel that was slain in the mountains of Gilboa; over those who were lovely and pleasant in their lives, and in their death were not divided, who were swifter than eagles and stronger than lions; over the mighty fallen in the midst of battle; over that friend whose love for him was wonderful, passing the love of women.*

"Now we will descend for the last time to the plain, this time to the main division of it. To the south of us are the hills of Samaria. Just at their foot is Jenîn, where we must spend the night. Now for a gallop. Come on; spur your horse, Harry. It's a splendid race-course!"

---

* 2 Sam. 1 : 17–27.

CHAPTER XXVI.

A NIGHT AT JENÎN.

LATE in the afternoon they were riding through a lane between two long lines of cactus-hedge. The place is the entrance to the village of Jenîn, the En-gannim of the Old Testament.* Will and Elias had been talking together. Now Will said to Harry,

"We are likely to have here the roughest night of the journey. We knew before that there was no hospice in the place, and Elias says there are only two houses fit for us to stay at. He thinks we can get into one of them if the owner is not away."

"I wonder if it will be worse than that night at Tyre?"

"Oh, I imagine so. Only 'worse' is hardly the word, for this is just what we have been wanting. We were in a native's house in Tyre; but the family was Christianized and lived partly in modern fashion. Here we will have to take the real, unmodified Syrian style, whatever it may

---

* The place is mentioned twice in Scripture: Josh. 19:21, and 21:29.

prove to be. I am glad of it. It will be interesting, but, I imagine, not comfortable. Is this the place, Elias?"

"Yes, sir."

"Well, knock at the gate."

"There is no seeing through or over the wall to find first what accommodations there are inside," said Harry. "It might be part of a fort. It looks as though they were afraid of being attacked."

"Very likely they do fear that. You notice all the houses are much the same. They are in an exposed place—so near to the plain and the roaming Bedouins."

The knock was answered; and after a little parleying between Elias and the man, Elias reported that they could stay there if they chose.

The top of the gateway was too low to ride under. They dismounted and led their horses into the yard of the establishment. At the further end of this walled yard, opposite the entrance, was the house, built of stone, with an arched dome-like roof. Harry pushed through the one small door to explore the inside. In a minute he was back.

"It doesn't take long to see all there is in there. There is only one room, with a slit in the wall on one side for a window, a clay floor, and two or three shelves. There's a sort of box on one side, the place of honor, I suppose, where we can spread our blankets for a bed. But the room is dreadfully close and damp. I would n't think any fresh air had been let in for a week, and the woman has just been pouring over the floor two or three jars of water. I suppose she wants to make it as clean for us as she can at short notice."

"Well, we might as well take possession and make ourselves at home. We will build a fire in the brazier and take it into the room. That will help get rid of some of the bad odors. Elias, ask them what they have here to eat."

Elias withdrew to a corner of the yard to which the man and woman had betaken themselves, and where they were cooking their own supper over a handful of coals.

In the meantime the horses had been fastened for the night, and the donkey with them, near the door of the house. The donkey's master had spread his rugs on the ground, and having squatted himself upon them, was soberly smoking, prepared to spend the night there rather than inside, wisely, as it proved.

Hassan, when he had fed the horses, found a place near him.

Elias returned and reported.

"They say you are welcome to the use of everything they have—house and rugs and wood and brazier and water—but they haven't a thing to eat excepting the native bread which they are cooking now."

"Come with us, then, into the village, and we will see what we can get. We ought to find a chicken and some eggs, at least. These you could cook."

They found the market-place and made their purchases. In roaming about the streets afterwards they came to a café, where a number of rough men, and among them several in uniform, were occupying low cane-bottomed stools around the door. They stopped and talked with the men. The soldiers were a part of a government patrol for the road towards Nablûs and Jerusalem. There was need of them, Elias said. They were heavily armed with swords and big horse-pistols, clumsy, but showing delicate workmanship on the richly-inlaid stocks. Will examined the weapons, and as he handed them back took from his pocket his own comparatively tiny revolver.

"That seems to astonish them," remarked Harry.

"They want to know how many times it will fire," said Elias, "and how far off it will kill."

"Ask them if that chicken up the path yonder is for sale."

"Yes, sir, it is."

Bang! bang! bang! bang!

"Go get it, Elias. How many times was it hit?" The men were examining it curiously.

"Four times they say, sir."

"It is very well to confirm the natives in these parts," said Will to Harry, as they walked back to their lodging-place, "in the idea which they have that we foreigners always go thoroughly armed, and that we would not be slow or unskilful in using our weapons if there were occasion for it."

They had good success in preparing their supper. It was inartistically cooked and roughly served, but that mattered nothing with appetites such as theirs. What remained after the feast Elias stored away under the open box that was to serve them as a bed, for lack, as he thought, of any safer place.

The travellers sat late that evening outside the door. They were in no haste to venture inside, where they had small hopes of spending a comfortable night. But finally they entered and lay down where they had arranged their shawls and blankets.

For a while there was a dim light from a flaring

candle. That went out, and then the place was dark as Egypt, excepting where a few red coals smouldered in a corner in the brazier. Soon they were dead too. There wasn't a glimmer, excepting as the starlight outside just showed the doorway.

Presently the partly-open door was swung a little farther, and they could see a dark shape glide through. Another and another followed, until there must have been a dozen men somewhere in the room! Who might they be? What was going on? There was no knowing. Whoever they were, they seemed, from the sounds, to spread their rugs on the floor and lie down and go to sleep. It was not likely there was any danger. They found afterwards there was none. The place was a sort of inn; but the situation was not helpful to sleep, if all else had been well. Half an hour passed.

"Are you asleep, Cousin Will?"

"No; good night."

Another half-hour or so; then,

"Cousin Will, are you asleep?"

"No."

"Well, are we two you and I, or are we somebody else? It seems as though we couldn't be ourselves. I never in my life was in so queer a place."

"Go to sleep."

A long silence; then softly,

"Cousin Will, are you asleep?"

"No, and not likely to be, I think."

"Did you hear that noise under us? What was it?"

"I do n't know; something stealing our chicken, I suppose—cats, most likely. It's too late to save it. Go to sleep if you can; I can't."

Another long silence; then softly once more, but very earnestly,

"Cousin Will, are you asleep?"

"No."

"Do you know—I've just thought—when that woman was soaking the floor after we came, I supposed she was trying to clean up for us. It was n't that. You know there's no other way to do it. She was soaking the fleas to keep them quiet; was n't she?"

"I've no doubt of it; and instead she drove them all, every one, right here to the only dry place they could find in the room. Good night; go to sleep."

"I'll try; but if I do I know I'll dream I'm on Mount Ararat, with fleas swimming in from everywhere. Good night."

With the very first sign of morning Will rose and made his way into the fresh air. (Harry was asleep at last.) He roused Hassan to feed the horses in a hurry, and Elias to get together what was left for breakfast.

When Harry appeared, very soon after, all was ready. They ate, paid their host, led out the horses, mounted, and rode off through the beautiful morning, drawing deep breaths of the sweet air, and gradually losing the feverishness of the night in the coolness and purity of the new day.

So they left Jenîn, gladly taking their way towards Nablûs through the "hill country of Samaria."

CHAPTER XXVII.

JENÎN TO NABLÛS.

For five hours they rode towards the south, through a region of very great beauty and interest. Sometimes the path was through green meadows and yellow fields of grain. Sometimes it led along the sides of the hills, so giving birds-eye views of the harvesters at work, either on the plains, cutting and loading their harvest, or about their villages, threshing and storing it. These villages are never located on the plain itself, but oftenest on the summits of little knolls. Sometimes, again, the path would lead straight up and over high hills, out of one valley into another. Then there would be grand distant views. Once especially it was so, when the Mediterranean and a bit of the Plain of Jaffa showed away off in the west, and at the same time, in the north, once more and for the last time, the white top of Mount Hermon.

"This is all far more than I anticipated," said Will; "more every way. I have read so many descriptions of travel here I thought that I could almost find my way alone, and that I knew just what the general aspect of the country would be. But it is not so. The valleys are deeper and more beautiful than I had any idea of; the mountains are higher and grander; the distances seem greater. There is more of richness and variety and fertility. It is as I would have it, for after this the land will always seem to me more as I would wish the home of the Saviour to seem. Palestine has been belittled in my thought; I suppose just because I have seen so many poor pictures and maps and little models of it.

"We are not far now from the site of Dothan. It is to the west of us, with fine pasture-lands about it to-day, as there were when Joseph's brethren led their flocks there and plotted to destroy the dreamer.* And later, you remember, it was there that Elisha was besieged by a Syrian army, until he prayed to God, and the Syrians were struck with blindness and led away to the king of Israel in Samaria.†

"The village just before us on the top of that knoll is Sanûr. It is strongly located. All this long plain which it commands in winter is a great lake. When it dries up in the spring they sow it, and see what rich harvests follow. Not far beyond is another similar town, Jeba. There the path we are to take to Samaria branches

* Gen. 37 : 17 ff. † 2 Kings 6 : 13 ff.

off to the right from the direct route to Nablûs."

In about five hours from Jenîn the travellers reached Sebustieh, the ancient city of Samaria, the capital of the Ten Tribes from the time of Omri* until the kingdom was destroyed in 721 B. C. and the people carried away captive into Assyria.

"If the glory of the old city was equal to the glory of its site," said Will, "it must have been one of the fairest cities of the world. The view from the top of this hill, six hundred feet above the valley, is a noted one, and certainly it is worthy of its reputation."

"And what a strong place it must have been when it was fortified. Think, Cousin Will, of an army having to fight its way up to where we are standing."

"Armies have tried to do that. The city has withstood terrible sieges. Once especially the famine and distress of every kind inside the walls were awful. The inhabitants were ready to eat human flesh in their hunger.† The Syrians tried twice to capture the city without success. But when the king of Assyria came and besieged it for three years it was forced to yield at last. That was the death-blow to the kingdom of Is-

* 1 Kings 16:23, 24.   B. C. 925.   † 2 Kings 6:24 ff.

rael. The Ten Tribes were carried away captive, and people of other nationalities were introduced to occupy the depopulated land.*

"Alexander the Great, John Hyrcanus, one of the Maccabees, and especially Herod the Great, all had more or less to do with the after-history of the place. Herod made it very beautiful with temples and colonnades and walls. Some of the ruins here belong to his time."

"How strange it seems," said Harry, "to see great columns like those yonder standing and lying about in a ploughed field almost as though the farmers had sowed a wrong sort of seed and these had come up instead of grain. They are as regularly placed as rows of corn."

"Altogether there are about one hundred and thirty of those carved and polished columns. At this spot on the summit of the hill it is very likely there was built a great temple to Baal. We know there was one somewhere hereabouts, which Jehu broke down after the slaying of the priests of Baal, when he was purifying the kingdom from the evils introduced by the house of Ahab."†

"There are no other ruins here of much account, excepting this interesting church of the time of the Crusaders, the 'Church of St. John.' It still shows traces of very graceful architecture.

* 2 Kings 18:9 ff.   † 2 Kings 10:17 ff.

And down one long flight of stairs there is a small room, with marble flooring laid in pretty mosaic, which shows on its walls even now the coats of arms of old crusading knights who lived, and it may be died here. We will examine the church, and then ride on to Nablûs."

About two hours later they were in the midst of another of the fairest scenes of Palestine; not now on the mountains, but between them. They were riding through the "Valley of Nablûs."

"Some travellers praise this valley as the most beautiful place in Palestine; and I am not sure but they are right," said Will.

"It reminds me of the approach to Damascus."

"Yes, it is much like that in the abundance of its rushing waters and the rich vegetation— trees and bushes and gardens and orchards and bits of meadow; but here the mountains crowd down on both sides of us as they do not there."

"The pass grows narrower and narrower."

"And just before reaching the narrowest part, between Mount Ebal and Gerizim, there lies Nablûs, the ancient Shechem, much the largest and most prosperous city that we have seen since leaving Beirût. Its population now is about five thousand."

Nablûs is a walled city. Soon they were riding through the gateway and along narrow and very slippery paved streets. They turned to the left, across a little bridge, and rode up to the large Latin hospice where for the last time they were to receive hospitality from the monks of Palestine.

As they examined the establishment Harry thought the prospect for the night was good, but only as compared with their previous night at Jenîn.

What remained of the daylight they used in wandering across the quaint city, through its narrow and often covered streets, past a few of the eighty springs that help to make the city and the valley beautiful, and a little way up the slope of Mount Gerizim beyond. The visited a plain Mohammedan mosque, and in another part of the city climbed the ruined tower of a little church set deep among groves of fig-trees and pomegranates and fragrant orange-trees. As they looked out and down upon the city, and up to the mountains on opposite sides, Harry said,

"It is so beautiful, suppose we stay here till dark. Can't we?"

"Yes," Will answered. "It is pleasanter here than in the hospice, and it is easier here to recall the wonderful things that have happened in the history of the place. For instance, imagine what the effect must have been when Jotham stood on these shelving rocks just above us, after Abimelech had slain all the others of Gideon's sons, and shouted to the people his warning against their making Abimelech king.*

"That was in the time of the Judges. Later it was here that the people gathered after the death of Solomon to choose his successor. Rehoboam expected to be king, but the Ten Tribes rejected him and chose Jeroboam instead. So the kingdom was divided.† Jerusalem remained the capital of Judah and Benjamin. This city for a while was the capital of the new confederacy.

"In the final overthrow of Israel by the Assyrians nearly all the Jews were removed from this region and foreigners brought in to take their place. That accounts for the hostility between the inhabitants of Judæa and the Samaritans. It showed itself again and again, both in the Old Testament history and in the New. The two people were not brethren. The one class were Jews, the other foreigners, or a mixture of foreigners and a few of the original inhabitants.

"Three hundred years before Christ the Samaritans built on Mount Gerizim a rival temple to that at Jerusalem. It was destroyed about

---

* Judges 9: 5 ff.   † 1 Kings 12: 16, 20.

B. C. 129; but the place is held sacred yet. The modern Samaritans—there are about one hundred and fifty of them—are holding one of their festivals there now. But of all the events that have ever happened here, the most imposing, by far, was the gathering between these two mountains of all the tribes of Israel, soon after they had entered the Promised Land. They had come to listen to the rehearsal of the law and to the solemn blessings and cursings which were shouted back and forth before the whole people from the slopes of the opposite mountains.* That was the most imposing event; but after all it is not the one which I love best to think about. Do you know what that is?

"It happened fifteen hundred years later, in the New Testament time, when Christ was journeying with his disciples by the same route that we are following, but in the opposite direction, from Jerusalem to Galilee. They came to the outskirts of the city, to 'Jacob's Well,' which we will see to-morrow, and being wearied with the day's journey, just as we sometimes are, he sat there, resting and awaiting his disciples, who had come into the city to buy food; and yet although he was weary and might easily have remained silent if he had chosen, he did not so choose.

* Deut. 27 : 11 ff.; Josh. 8 : 33 ff.

Instead he spoke words to the Samaritan woman which not merely helped her and her friends, but have helped you and me, Harry—have helped the whole world. To my thought, nothing of greater moment than that ever happened in the region of Nablûs."

When the sun had set in the twilight, Will and Harry walked back across the city to their night's lodging-place. As they entered, a small congregation was gathering in the chapel of the convent for the evening service. They joined the company, and there silently in their own way they worshipped God, while the responses and the rude music of the choristers and the mumbled reading and recitation of the priest went on monotonously about them.

"Elias, to-morrow night we must be in Jerusalem."

"It will be a very long day's ride, sir."

"I know it will. Tell Hassan to be ready with the horses by sunrise, or a little before."

"Yes, sir;" and Elias withdrew.

"I imagine," said Harry, "there would have been rebellion over that, except for what the men learned at Acre."

"Very likely. Travellers usually make two stages between Nablûs and Jerusalem."

CHAPTER XXVIII.

NABLÛS TO JERUSALEM.

At four o'clock the travellers rode through the court of the convent and turned into the path leading towards Jerusalem. It was still dark. The sky was overcast, the air chilly. Ebal and Gerizim showed dimly on either side, and closed in upon them nearer and nearer as they rode towards the east, until in the narrowest place the two were hardly more than sixty rods apart. It was light by the time they reached "Jacob's Well," a mile or two from the city.

"There is scarcely any doubt," said Will, that this is really the well which Jacob dug when he came with his flocks from Padan-aram to sojourn in the land of the Canaanites, and that it was here that the Saviour sat and talked with the woman of Sychar. When she spoke of the mountain in which her forefathers worshipped, and when Christ said, 'The hour cometh when ye shall neither in this mountain, nor yet at Jerusalem, worship the Father,' no doubt they looked to the mountain yonder and the Samaritan temple, whose ruins can yet be seen. There is little of interest about the place now excepting for its associations. The well is so filled with rubbish that there is no chance of careful examination of it; but we know from the reports of other travellers that it was cut evenly through the solid rock, with a diameter of nine feet and a depth of at least one hundred and five feet."

By nine o'clock the clouds had disappeared after a few drops of rain had fallen, rare enough at this season in Palestine. During the rest of the day the sun blazed with intense heat, especially where the path led, as it often did, over long reaches of bare rock. The hot sirocco blew also from the south.

They camped at noon in a grove of olives near the "Robbers' Cave," a place of doubtful reputation in former times and not over safe, Elias thought, even now. They made but a short nooning. The air in the valley under the trees was almost stifling, and motion through it, even on horseback, was more comfortable than the dead stillness.

"Cousin Will, did you ever see anywhere as mean a road as this? The fields on each side seem clear enough; if we could get up into them it would be easier going; but here! It seems as though they had chosen the washed-out bed of a brook for the roadway, and then had cleared their land by pitching all the round pebble-stones they could find over into it."

"That is just what they have done. I don't know about the brook; I should think there might be a rush of water here during the winter rains; but the farmers do really clear their fields at times at the expense of the paths."

"It doesn't seem as if the horses could keep their feet over them. They couldn't excepting as they go like snails. The white donkey does better."

Up and down, through valleys and over bare mountain ridges, close along the sides of hills, up and down, but for the most part gradually ascending, they rode until late in the afternoon, when they drew near to Jerusalem. They were approaching from the north; their first view would be from Mount Scopus. They rode rapidly ahead of the men. A few minutes more, and they would look down upon the Holy City! At last they saw it, the central city of the world. They dismounted, and holding their horses by the bridles, looked long in silence upon the picture before them. The silence was broken by Will.

"In truth," he said, "it is the 'central city of the world.' I like the figure which the old rabbinical writers used. 'The whole world,' they said, 'is an eye; the white of the eye is the ocean surrounding the land; the black iris is the dry land; the pupil is Jerusalem; and the image in the pupil is the temple.'*

"It is easy to recognize the different localities in and about the city. This Mount Scopus, to the north, rises 2,715 feet above the level of the Mediterranean. It was here that Titus made his headquarters during the siege of Jerusalem in the year 70. There to the east of the city is the Mount of Olives. We must go there to-morrow. Between it and the walls is the 'Valley of Jehoshaphat,'† with the brook Kidron; and meeting this almost at right angles to the south of the city is the 'Valley of Hinnom.'

"Inside the walls, which are for the most part of the time of the Crusaders, the one object prominent above the crowded houses is the beautiful 'Dome of the Rock.' It occupies part of the temple area on Mount Moriah. Mount Zion is opposite, with the great 'Tower of David' by the Jaffa Gate.

"We shall have time for nearer views of these places before we leave the city, though no more time than we shall need, if we take the next steamer from Jaffa for home. We want to

---

* "Otho Lex," p. 266.
† This is not the valley mentioned in the prophecy of Joel, chapter 3: 2, 12.

JERUSALEM.

take that steamer, for every one tells us it is getting too hot to stay here much longer."

They rode on down the slope of the bare hill towards the city. Half a mile from the walls they came to the "Tombs of the Kings."

"It would take but a few minutes, and would save our coming again, if we stopped now to explore these tombs," said Will.

They found a doorway in the high board fence with which the present owners have surrounded the place. The keeper received them. Candles were lighted, and stooping as they went, they crept through the narrow passages. The work was more elaborate and on a larger scale than anything of the kind they had yet seen. There is an outer court sunk in the solid rock about ninety feet square and twenty feet deep. On one side runs a long portico, with columns in the centre. A very low entrance-way at the end of the portico leads into a dark ante-chamber nineteen feet square and seven or eight feet high. Out of this there are three passages leading into other rooms, which contain crypts for the sarcophagi and bodies of the dead. From one of the rooms another passage leads down into a large vault with more crypts along its sides. All the excavations were made in exceedingly hard rock. It was so long and difficult a work, it seems as though only kings were likely to have undertaken it. Probably that is one reason for the name, "Tombs of the Kings." The doors have disappeared now, but they were of stone, hung on stone hinges.

It was a pleasant contrast, as Harry and Will came out into the light, to see two pet gazelles playing and feeding on the grass; and it was a contrast again to find outside the inclosing fence all the grove and the paths towards the city filled with crowds of gayly-dressed people, of every age and condition, hastening towards their homes. It was some festival time, and they were returning from the day's merry-making.

The travellers passed through the wall at the Damascus Gate, and at once were in the narrow, busy, slippery streets of Jerusalem. The goal was reached. Their horseback-ride through Palestine was ended. All they would do now would be to make short excursions in and near the city. After a few days they would go down by stage to Jaffa in time to embark by the next steamer.

They found comfortable lodgings at the German hotel. The servants were dismissed—Elias without regret and with only his pay, Hassan with a liberal backsheesh. With two or three exceptions Hassan had done remarkably well. He was a quick, jovial, steady little fellow, and efficient in his department. The white donkey (none the worse for his journey) and his master, benefited by his visit to the springs of Tiberias, had parted from them as they neared the city.

It was time to rest. They were thoroughly tired with the day's ride. They had been in the saddle twelve hours. They might dream of the Holy City, but they could see no more of it until the morrow.

CHAPTER XXIX.

AROUND JERUSALEM.

"It seems good to be where there are mails again," said Harry, as he and Will sat reading their letters before going out to explore the city.

Their plan this morning was to ride first to Bethlehem.

Isa, their new guide, soon arrived with the horses; but they preferred walking as far as the Jaffa Gate; the streets were too steep and slippery for safe riding.

Outside the gate they mounted, and keeping to the left, rode past bare fields, between walls of flint stone, over rough roads, to the south.

After an hour and a half they neared Bethlehem. The distant view of the town above its terraced hills was very attractive, worthy of the thoughts it suggested to the travellers of Ruth and Naomi and David and the Saviour, and the songs of angels and listening shepherds; but the town itself is not in keeping. It seems too modern, too busy and bustling and selfish, ever to have been the birthplace of the Prince of Peace. And to make it worse, as they entered the gates they found there had just been a fight with a neighboring village in regard to a piece of land. Prisoners had been brought in, and now the government soldiers had arrived to enforce order.

"I wanted it to be still and quiet and beautiful here," said Harry, "with the people going about as though they knew they were in a sacred place, and feeling and showing a kindly spirit, with all the women like Raphael's Marys, and the men as sedate as Joseph, and the children little angels. They're far from that. I'd like to make these young rascals understand that when we say we don't want their curiosities we mean it. What a shouting lot of them there are! As to the women, they are not Marys, but they are fairly handsome, or rather, are less ugly than most that we have seen. It seems not to be the fashion here to tattoo their faces; and their coin head-dresses and rings and bracelets are rather becoming."

They reached the "Church of the Nativity," a great rambling, irregular pile. In fact, it is three churches under one roof—Latin, Greek, and Armenian.

"Look there, Harry! Do you see that Turkish soldier lolling on the pavement? He is stationed here to keep the priests of the different churches from quarrelling—from fighting with each other. The same thing has to be done in other places. It is done even in the 'Church of the Holy Sepulchre' in Jerusalem, especially during the time of the Easter pilgrimages."

They were conducted to all the traditional "holy places"—to the "Cave of the Nativity," to the manger, to the cell in which St. Jerome spent many years while at work on his translation of the Bible, to his tomb.

When they had completed the survey they left the church, and soon after rode again through the arched gateway of the walls and along the narrow hill-path back to Jerusalem.

In the afternoon they visited Bethany. Leaving the city by the Damascus Gate, they followed the line of walls around to the right as far as St. Stephen's Gate, facing the Mount of Olives.

From this gate the path descends steeply to the level of the brook Kidron, in the valley of Jehoshaphat. They crossed its dry bed, and at once began the ascent of the Mount of Olives. They passed the walls of the Garden of Gethsemane on their right without stopping, planning to delay there on their return from Bethany. When they reached the summit, they turned and looked long and thoughtfully over the impressive view before them.

"To my mind," said Will, "the sight of Jerusalem from this point is more satisfying than from any other place. The deep ravine between us and the city walls, and the nearness of the temple area with its mosques, help the effect greatly; and perhaps the thought of the times the Saviour rested here on his way to and from Bethany has something to do with it. We are one hundred feet above the highest part of the city, and five hundred and fifty feet above the brook Kidron in the bed of the valley. But look the other way, Harry, to the east."

Harry looked, and exclaimed with surprise.

"Why, I had no thought," he said, "of seeing so plainly the Dead Sea and the mountains of Moab."

"Nor had I; but there certainly are the mountains, and there is the wonderful sea shining in the sun, four thousand feet below us, like a sheet of silver. Do you notice the light haze over the water? It tells even at this distance something of what the intense heat there must be. No wonder we are told that it is too hot now safely to go there. And then such a tumbling together as there is of hills and valleys nearer to us, between us and Bethany! I had supposed there was an easy, even slope from where we stand down towards the village; that it was quiet scenery, rather than bold and beautiful, through which the Saviour passed in his morning and evening walks between Jerusalem and the house of Lazarus. But this is bold, and it is exceedingly beautiful even now when there is scarcely anything excepting natural beauty of location to make it attractive; no woods now, no pleasant villages, no quiet, happy homes, as there once were when Christ passed here to and from Jerusalem.

"Have you ever thought, Harry, why it was that the Saviour loved to rest so often in Bethany?—not because they were wiser or richer or nobler in Lazarus' home than in other places, but just because there he was certain always of a loving welcome. And if that was so, if it was that which made this home a dear Bethany to him, how many other Bethanys there ought to be in the world, home Bethanys and heart Bethanys also, where Christ will be so loved and welcomed that he will enter in, not for a night, as he used to do there, but to abide always! His brief visits were glad times to Martha and Mary and Lazarus. It is by having our hearts Bethanys, and Christ abiding in them, that we can best be glad and strong, Harry; true men, pure and unselfish, noblemen every way, because Christlike. Think how it would be if every place in the world, every little hamlet, every home, every heart, was that way! Well, all we can do is to see that our own hearts, and as many others as we can reach, are Bethanys."

They were in no haste to descend from the summit of the mountain. Presently Harry broke a long silence.

"Cousin Will, do you remember, away back—it seems a long time ago—the evening before we left home, at prayers father read the one hundred and twenty-fifth Psalm?"

"Yes, the Psalm which declares that as the mountains are round about Jerusalem, so the Lord is round about his people from henceforth even for ever."

"And I said how strange it seemed to think that before long I should see those mountains; and now we do see them."

"And to me," said Will, "those verses will always have a deeper meaning than heretofore; for I had thought of 'the mountains,' whose protection is compared to that of God, as being simply one line of hills encircling the city like a line of encamped soldiery. But how much more there is than that! Instead of one line of mountains, there is camp after camp of them about the city as far as we can see; and not in one direction only, but we can see them towards the Jordan and beyond and to the south, and we came over them all the way from the Plain of Esdraelon in the north, and on the west they reach to the Plain of Jaffa. Indeed, if God is 'round about' one like that, a man is safe, absolutely safe, always."

They turned from the summit and rode for a mile and more among the hills down to Bethany. Eager boys followed them as they entered the village, and when they dismounted stood ready to hold their horses and to show them the "Tomb of Lazarus" and the "House of Simon the Leper."

Though there is no probability that the dark passage-way of forty steps or so, down which they went with lighted tapers, is the place of the great miracle,* and none that the ruined house was ever the scene of the feast where Mary broke the alabaster box of ointment and anointed Christ for his burial,† and though the rude huts have nothing suggestive of the home that Jesus loved, still it was not hard to imagine a different scene, a beautiful, shaded village with quiet streets, and with the one home especially in it that was dearest of all to the Saviour, because always he was certain there of a loving welcome from those who had learned of him and chosen the better part. It was not hard to imagine that Bethany.

They mounted their horses and rode back towards Jerusalem, following now the main road

* John 11.   † Matt. 26:6.

from the Jordan and Jericho along the southern side of Olivet. As the road curved to the right around the mountain, suddenly in full view before them lay the Holy City. They had come to the very place where Christ stood with his disciples when in his sympathy and love he mourned over the city and exclaimed in infinite tenderness, "O Jerusalem, Jerusalem, which killest the prophets, and stonest them that are sent unto thee; how often would I have gathered thy children together, as a hen doth gather her brood under her wings, and ye would not!"*

At the foot of the mountain they turned aside to visit the Garden of Gethsemane. The traditional spot is inclosed now with a high wall of stone, which effectually hides from the passers-by the whole interior. They were admitted by the keeper. Within they found a carefully-cultivated garden of brilliantly-blooming flowers, laid out in regularly-formed beds and fenced inclosures. If that had been all, the impressions could only have been unpleasant, out of harmony with the thoughts suggested by the name Gethsemane; but it was not all. Among the flowers there stood old, old olive-trees, so hoary and reverend, and so in keeping with one's thoughts of the solemn grove where Christ wept and prayed before the

* Luke 13 : 34.

crucifixion, that at once they drew and held the attention. And underneath one of these ancient olives, seated on a rude bench, was an old, old monk, reading, and so absorbed in the little book which he held that he seemed not to know that the travellers were there as they passed before him. It was perhaps the story of the Garden that he was reading. So when they went away from the inclosure their feelings were not wholly different from what they would have been if the place had remained unchanged by the hands of men through the centuries and they had known it to be the real Gethsemane.

Instead of going north towards the Damascus Gate, they turned now to the south and rode along the Valley of Jehoshaphat.

"You will be surprised," said Will, "at the number of graves and tombs along these valleys. This slope on our right, below the temple area, is considered a most sacred place. All Mohammedans desire to be buried here. And opposite on our left is another cemetery of the Jews. Look just above the Moslem burying-ground. Do you see a large stone there built out from the city wall?"

"Yes."

"There is a foolish tradition which declares that at the resurrection the judgment-seat will be by that stone, and that as the dead rise from these many graves they will at once be required, as a test, to pass along a line stretched from the stone across the valley. Only the good will succeed. The wicked will fall and be lost.

"Farther south you see other tombs on the left. They are certainly very ancient, but their full history is not known. One of them is called the Tomb of Jehoshaphat, another of Absalom, another of St. James, another of Zechariah. That of Absalom has the appearance of a miniature temple; those of Jehoshaphat and St. James are rock caves, much like others which we have seen. Zechariah's is curiously formed by cutting away the original rock until only the monument is left."

They passed the "Fountain of the Virgin," with a long flight of steps leading down to the water, and the "Pool of Siloam," and the village of Siloam along the cliffs on the left, and the "King's Gardens."

From the Valley of Jehoshaphat they turned west into the Valley of Hinnom. They saw more cemeteries, and the "Potter's Field" that was bought with the thirty pieces of silver which Judas returned to the Sanhedrin after he had betrayed his Lord.*

* Matt. 27:3 ff.

Entering the Valley of Hinnom from the north, and lying between Mount Moriah and Mount Zion, is the Valley of the Tyropœon. This valley is filled now, in large part—as to some extent are all the valleys about Jerusalem— with the accumulated rubbish of the city's centuries of peace and war, of destruction and rebuilding.

"We will explore that valley to-morrow," said Will. "Now we will go on to the south and west of Mount Zion, towards the Jaffa Gate."

"Do look there, Cousin Will! Isn't that terrible!" exclaimed Harry. "They must be lepers!"

They had come to a part of the road where these miserable people congregate to beg of the passers-by. Hospitals have been provided for them, but many prefer not to occupy them. They pressed after the travellers, not offering to touch them, but exhibiting their maimed limbs, crying and muttering. It was pitiable in the extreme.

The "Tower of David" was now a near and a conspicuous landmark before them. Very soon they reached it. Just beyond is the Jaffa Gate, and there they reëntered the city. They had completed the circuit of the walls. Giving their horses to Isa, they found their way on foot, closely attended a good part of the distance by a most persistent beggar, down the narrow streets to their lodgings.

It had been a crowded day, and, for the most part, a very satisfactory one. The impression left by their visit to Bethlehem was not wholly pleasant, but the unpleasant parts could not destroy the charm of the thought that it was there that so much which was beautiful and blessed had occurred. The one thought that it was even there, under those very skies, that the dear child Jesus was born was enough to thrill them then; and they did not forget it when they had returned to their Western homes. It was some months later, near Christmas-time, that one day Harry received a letter from Cousin Will inclosing this:

UNDER A STAR.

K. W. N.

Un - der a star in the Ho - ly Land
Li - eth a child in the mother's arms. "Sleep," she sings, "sleep,

ba - by, sleep,   Angels will guard thee from all   a - larms."

 Under that star from the distant East
  Journey the magi with gifts for a king.
 Unto whom do wise men thus
  Presents of gold and of incense bring?

 Under the stars the shepherds watch,
  Keeping their flocks in the silver light.
 Hark! the angel choirs proclaim,
  "Christ is the King who is born to-night!"

 Here in the homes of a Western clime,
  Under the stars let our music ring,
 While to him, that Saviour-king,
  Offerings the richest—our hearts—we bring.

DOME OF THE ROCK.

CHAPTER XXX.

SACRED SITES.

"THIS morning we are to visit the 'Haram Area,' the site of the old Jewish temple on the summit of Mount Moriah in the southeast corner of the city. Not long ago it would have been impossible to explore the place, as we can easily do now with a pass from the officials and an official guard."

"We have had fine views of the area from a distance," said Harry. "Now I am curious to find what it is like close by."

Upon reaching the entrance they were admitted without trouble to what the Mohammedans as well as the Jews consider one of the most sacred places in the world. It is the most sacred place, next to Mecca, the Mohammedans say. Mohammed taught that a single prayer offered here is equal to a thousand offered elsewhere.

Near the centre of the Haram Area rises a most beautiful structure. It is the "Dome of the Rock."* Outside and in it is rich with marble-work and tiles and stained glass and gold.

* Kubbet es-Sakhrah.

"I had always supposed it to be a rather plain building," said Harry, as they stood before it, "of interest mostly because of its location and peculiar architecture; but instead it is like a beautiful bouquet of well-arranged flowers."

"It would certainly be easy to find here all the prominent colors of flowers," said Will. "There is variety enough in the mosaics alone for that."

Flights of stairs lead to a platform, partly paved in marble, 550 feet in length from north to south, and 450 feet in width. At the centre of this platform is built the beautiful domed octagon around and over the sacred rock, which rock, tradition says, was the threshing-floor of "Araunah the Jebusite," where David sacrificed in the time of the great plague; the site also of the altar of sacrifice in Solomon's temple; and later still, the place from which Mohammed ascended into Paradise. All that and more is claimed for it. The diameter of the octagon is 170 feet. Each side measures 67 feet in length and is 46 feet high. These walls are laid in marble mosaic of rich patterns and colors, and with the roof are also ornamented with glazed tiles, many of them of a bright blue color. From the roof of this first story rises another wall, which is pierced near the top with windows that light the interior; and above the whole, 40 feet in height and 65 feet in diameter, cased in lead and crowned with a golden crescent, rests the "dome." The whole altitude, including the platform, is 170 feet. The interior is even richer than the outside, with its circles of marble columns and niches and mosaic pavement. The "rock" is cream-colored limestone, irregular in shape, about 57 feet long in the longest part, and 43 feet wide. It is protected from any touch, and in part from sight also, by a close iron fence.

The guide led them by a narrow passage-way underneath the rock, to show them, he said, how it was suspended between earth and heaven. The apparent supports at the sides, he explained, were only light masonry, with no strength of themselves to keep the rock in place. A hole in the rock roof of the cave he also explained as having been caused by the head of Mohammed when he passed there on his way to Paradise.

Another of his stories was concerning some silver nails in a part of the pavement under the dome. He said they marked the number of periods through which the world would continue to exist. Originally there were nineteen nails; now there are but three left; and these three would have been removed long ago and the world destroyed, excepting that Satan, who had stolen away the others and was removing these also, was discovered just in time, and driven off by the angel Gabriel!*

A few rods from the "Dome of the Rock," at the end of a line of delicate arches, is a very graceful carved pulpit, with a flight of steps leading up to it.

Farther on, in the very southern part of the area, is a large rambling mosque, or rather collection of mosques, the Mosque El Aksa, the Mosque of Omar,† with small grotesque columns beside the shrine, the Mosque of Abu Seka. Near by are the so-called "Stables of Solomon," great underground excavations, with many ancient columns. They noticed in one place an iron grating covered with shreds of cloth. It was another sacred place. It reminded them of the tree of offering they had seen near Tiberias, covered with rags—the "witches' tree," as Harry had called it.

At one part of the wall, near the closed golden gateway, they mounted to the battlements and

---

* It is uncertain when the "Dome of the Rock" was built; probably in the seventh century, and perhaps by the Caliph Omar.

† The "Dome of the Rock" is often called the "Mosque of Omar," but incorrectly. Strictly it is not a mosque at all, for there is no shrine towards Mecca; but one of the four portals opens in that direction.

rested there a while, looking off over the Valley of Jehoshaphat towards the Mount of Olives.

"All here is very quiet and peaceful now," said Will. "Even that little bird is not afraid to hop about the walls. But many and many a time, instead of little birds flying safely, there have been piles of dead bodies here, and crowds of men, sometimes fighting hand to hand, sometimes defending the walls from foes outside.

"Think of that one time among the many, hardly forty years after the Saviour died, when the Romans stormed this height and burned the temple! They had gained a part of the city. Titus was planning for a final assault the next morning, and he had given orders not to burn the holy place. But when night came the Jews made a fierce sally. They were repulsed. Then it was that one of the pursuing soldiers without orders flung a torch through a gilded door into the temple chambers. All at once they were in flames. It was a signal for the wildest excitement and for fierce and general renewal of the battle.

"Titus could not restrain his furious legions. They fell upon the people crowded here in the temple area, and slew them by thousands. They lay in heaps about the altars; the steps of the temple ran with blood; 6,000 women and children and unarmed men were burned to death in one of the cloisters!

"When it had all ended, when the soldiers, who had been like madmen, were restrained, and when the rest of the city was occupied and Titus had been saluted as victor and Cæsar, then the number of the slain was known: 1,100,000 Jews had fallen in the war; 97,000 were prisoners!

"And yet now, as I said, it seems as though it had always been as quiet and as safe here as it is for us and the birds to-day. I suppose there is no other city in the world which has known in its time as much misery and suffering as has fallen to the lot of Jerusalem.

"But we must go. We want to see the old foundation-stones of these walls and the Jews' 'Wailing-Place,' in the Tyropœon Valley, and Robinson's Arch.'"

When they had dismissed the numerous attendants and left the Haram Area, Isa led them by hot and narrow and filthy streets through the Jews' quarter, until they reached a somewhat wider, quiet inclosure, a few rods in length, with a common stone wall on one side, and overshadowed on the other by the high, ancient foundations of the temple area. It is the Jews' "Wailing-Place." From all parts of the world Jewish pilgrims come to sit here before the high,

JEWS' WAILING-PLACE.

bevelled stones, or to lean lovingly against them, while they bewail the desolation that has fallen upon Zion. Without doubt some of these stones were placed where they now are as long ago as in the time of Herod, and possibly the date was much earlier.

Not far south of the Wailing-Place, in the Tyropœon Valley, is a bit of ruin called "Robinson's Arch." As they stood beside it Will said,

"This has always seemed to me one of the most interesting relics about Jerusalem. Lately Lieut. Warren, of the Palestine Exploring Expedition, has made further examinations and further discoveries in regard to it. It was known from historical records that a great bridge once reached across this valley, connecting Mount Moriah and Mount Zion. The bridge was here as late as the time of the Romans. Titus stood on it to confer with the Jews in the temple after he had captured Mount Zion. But every sign of the structure had at last disappeared, unless this bit of arch was a part of it. Dr. Robinson believed it was a part. And he was right; for Lieut. Warren has found, directly opposite across the valley, the other end of the bridge—a buttress of great stones built against the side of Mount Zion. When he had found that, he thought he ought to find also, between these ends, some remains of the rest of the fallen arch and the floor of the bridge. So he began digging again. He dug fifty feet below the present level of the valley before he was through the accumulated rubbish.

"Then he found what he was in search of—some remains of the great bridge itself. There could be no doubt in regard to it; the shapes of the stones which he had uncovered were what they must have been to correspond with the curve of the first arch as estimated from the fragments at the end. It was a splendid bridge. The width of its roadway was upwards of fifty feet, the span of each supporting arch was forty-one feet, and some of the single stones weighed at the least twenty tons. Titus ordered it broken down.

"Now we will go back to the hotel, and after dinner we will visit the 'Church of the Holy Sepulchre.'"

In the afternoon, as they descended the few steps which lead into the court in front of the Church of the Holy Sepulchre, Will remarked concerning the place,

"This much we know: that for sixteen centuries this spot has been held in highest esteem as the site of the crucifixion and burial of our Lord. As long ago as the time of the Emperor Constantine and his mother St. Helena, a church, or monument of some sort, was erected to mark the spot. The present church is the finest in the city, and, as far as we know, is finer than were any of its predecessors. It took the place in 1808 of one that was destroyed by fire."

"But how very old and dingy parts of the outside look: and this stone pavement, how worn it is!" said Harry.

"Yes, the pavement is worn smooth by the thousands of pilgrims who come here every year, especially during the Easter festivals. Only a part of the wide doorway is open for the few visitors, but we are free to enter. Inside we shall find such a bewildering collection of chambers and cells and caves and stairways and galleries it would be foolish to try to trace them all. There are some seventy different 'stations' which the priests would show if we cared to see them. Here, as at Bethlehem, one roof covers the whole; and here also soldiers have to be always on guard to keep peace between the priests of the different sects.

"Here on our right, as we enter, is a chamber with the tombs of the Crusaders Baldwin and Godfrey. Next to it is the 'Chapel of Adam.' What do you suppose they say caused this split in the rock of the wall?"

"I've no idea," said Harry.

"The earthquake at the time of the crucifixion! Up these stairs is the 'Chapel of Calvary;' and here they show in the rock three holes, one of them with a silver covering, where they claim the crosses of the Saviour and of the thieves were set."

They descended to the first floor again and found near the entrance, midway between "Calvary" and the "Sepulchre," the "Stone of Unction," where the body of the Saviour was laid for its anointing before the burial, according to the tradition. Then they entered between two large buttresses into the imposing rotunda of the church, in the centre of which is the beautiful marble "Chapel of the Sepulchre." Within this chapel there is first the "Room of the Angels" who watched at the door of the sepulchre—and a piece of rock is shown as a part of the great stone which they rolled from the mouth of the tomb. Then comes a low passage, opening into what is to the pilgrim the holiest of holy places—a chamber about six feet square and seven feet high, in the middle of which is the tomb, covered with a marble slab. Possibly it is the very place in the garden of Joseph of Arimathæa where the body of the dear Saviour was laid, dead at last after the agony of Gethsemane and Calvary; but the weight of evidence is against it.

When they turned from the Sepulchre it was

nearly dark; but they wandered through the gorgeously-decorated Greek portion of the church, and to one and another of the minor shrines, until it was time to close the doors for the night.

As they walked homeward Harry said, "I wish there was some way of knowing how true the traditions are—whether any of these places are the real places."

"The chief of the traditions are certainly very old," answered Will. "That alone is enough to make them interesting. Whether or not the claims they make can possibly be true depends in large part upon what the position was of the ancient walls of the city. The crucifixion and the entombment we know were outside of the city limits; therefore if the line of the ancient walls was outside of the site of the church, as the present walls are, the traditions are false. But if the line was inside, some of them may be true. That has been a difficult question to determine; but the best authority now is against the traditions."

CHAPTER XXXI.

FROM JERUSALEM TO JAFFA.

"Do you remember, Harry, the other day we noticed near the Damascus Gate a low, dark opening in the rock under the wall above a heap of rubbish?"

"Yes, like the mouth of a cave."

"We must spend a little while in there this morning."

They walked to the Damascus Gate. Outside the wall, a few rods to the east, they found the entrance which they sought to the great subterranean quarries that are known to exist under a large part of Jerusalem. They had provided themselves with candles. These they lighted as soon as they entered.

"Had we planned for any extended exploration in here," said Will; "it would have been safest to have brought compasses and lines as well as candles. It is an easy place for losing one's self. When Dr. Barclay a few years ago discovered, or rediscovered the place, he found in an out-of-the-way part a skeleton, probably of some former careless explorer."

JAFFA.

"That isn't reassuring," remarked Harry. "Isa, don't you lead us too far away from that bright hole yonder where we came in. It looks a good distance off already."

"We will be careful," said Will.

"My! what was that?" exclaimed Harry, as something swept by him in the darkness with a rush and a whirr.

"Bats," said Isa. "There are hundreds of them here. It's a fine place for them."

Gradually descending, they wound their way among great supporting columns farther and farther from the entrance. The first chamber is 750 feet long, and the roof 30 feet high. Underneath, the floor is covered with heaps of rubbish, fallen stone and chippings from the rock. In places they could see nothing of the roof, only the pitchy darkness above and all about them. Other galleries and chambers open beyond.

"When Titus captured Jerusalem," said Will, "some of the Jews who had been fighting inside the walls on Mount Moriah mysteriously disappeared. Very likely it was into caverns such as these, and perhaps connected with these, that they escaped. Whether they ever found their way out I don't know."

"There it is again, about people coming in

here to die! Say, Cousin Will, let us get out of this, any way."

"Why?"

"Haven't you seen enough? I have, a plenty."

"Yes; and the rest I suppose would show nothing different. We will go home. Lead the way."

"I lead the way! I can't! I'm as turned about as though I was a top. I haven't the remotest idea which way is out. Cousin Will, it isn't pleasant here. It's not merely getting lost, but I'm thinking besides, what if a few tons more of this earth and stone were all ready to come down, and are only waiting to start until we walk under and jar it a trifle! It might put our candles out, you know, and dampen the matches too much to light them again. Why don't you turn around and start for the outside! I might begin to get nervous after a while if you don't. But what is that light ahead? Are there two entrances to this?"

"No," said Will, "only one. The light that you see is where we entered. We have been on our way out for a good while."

"Well, well!" exclaimed Harry, "I think I was turned about. I feel as though I must be looking from the wrong side of my head, or walking backwards. However, I'm very glad to get here without having those rocks put our candles out and spoil our matches."

There was but little more to see or to do in Jerusalem. They walked often about the streets, observing the busy life there; they visited again and again the places of chief interest; they wrote the last letters home, telling how nearly ended their time in Palestine was and when they expected to sail. The day came to pack their small amount of luggage. They were ready for the Jaffa stage.

About four o'clock that afternoon a porter took the baggage to the west gate. They followed on foot. The "stage" was waiting. It was a small, strongly-built wagon such as alone could be dragged safely over the exceedingly rough road and the steep hills between Jerusalem and the Plain of Sharon.

By nine o'clock the roughest of the riding was accomplished. They had reached Latrone, near the edge of the great plain, a town famous in the history of the Maccabees. They rested for an hour and then rode on again, hour after hour, in the darkness towards the "Great Sea." They were crossing the fertile land on the north of Philistia the home of the Philistines, those deadly foes of the Israelites.

"We are taking the same journey," said Will, "that was so often taken in Old Testament and in New Testament times, and is taken still by thousands every year; for Jaffa always has been, and is still, the chief seaport of Jerusalem. There is talk now of a railroad between the two cities. It would be easy to build it where we are riding, but difficult through the mountains."

On and on they rode, hour after hour, mile after mile. Presently the moon rose and helped them to pass the time by giving them a dim panorama of moonlit pictures. Will took the reins to warm himself and to keep awake. Then for a while they made better progress. At last they reached the edge of the wonderful orchards of Jaffa, which surround the city for miles; but so wide are they that still on and on they rode, through the fragrant avenues of trees, for another hour before they reached the city walls.

The sun was just rising when, thoroughly wearied, they dismounted from the stage at the hotel door. After resting half the forenoon they sallied out to walk through the busy, Oriental-like town of Jaffa and to stand again beside the familiar sea. From a distance Jaffa is a picturesque place, built as it is on a rocky promontory and with many of its streets so steep that the roofs of the lower houses are nearly on a level with the doors of those above. They came presently to the sea wall in front of the town.

"And this," said Will, as they stood looking off over the water, "is one of the three best harbors on the coast; and yet you see that even here there is no shelter whatever excepting for the smallest craft. They can get in past the reefs; but large ships must either go by without stopping, or risk anchoring outside in the open roadstead, just as that steamer yonder has done. She must be the 'Juno' on which we are to sail to-night. There is a small boat coming in now loaded from the ship. Do you see it?"

"Yes, and it seems to be driving with the wind straight towards the white water on those reefs! If they come much nearer they can't work clear of them. I don't believe they can do it any way! There! They are right on them. They will upset!"

But the next minute the boat was sweeping through a narrow channel that could scarcely be seen, clear of the rocks, but with the foam breaking close on either side. Once inside the reefs, and it was safe, in comparatively still water.

"I am sorry there is so much wind for us to-day," said Harry. "I hope it will go down by evening."

"And so do I," answered Will. "If it is

much worse we cannot safely get off to the ship. There are more accidents here, by far, than on all the rest of the coast together. Sometimes it is so rough that even the steamships do not venture to anchor."

At last the time had come for leaving Palestine. Very soon the "Juno" would weigh anchor and steam for Egypt. They must go on board. Though the wind had not gone down, there was a crowd of boats at the landing ready to take them off. They chose one. The baggage was put in the bows. They took their places at the stern. The word was given, and the men rowed out against the wind and the waves.

It was very rough. Down they would go into the trough of the sea out of sight, then up towards the sky, to balance there on the curve of the wave, and then over just in time to escape the breaking edge of foam. Then there would be a smoother reach for a few strokes, then the great waves again, large enough to have swamped them but for the care of the skilful boatmen.

But by far the most dangerous time would be when the boat reached the ship, and Will knew it. He said nothing at first when Harry wondered how in the world they were to get on board the "Juno" from such a rolling support as their boat; but as they neared the ship, he said,

"Now, Harry, if you were ever careful and quick in your life, be careful and quick here. You see the ship's steps hanging at the gangway with rope supports at the sides, and the lower platform deep in the water for a moment, and out again with every wave that passes. What you have to do at the word, when our boat rises, is to seize those ropes. If there is time before the boat sinks, step to the platform; but if not, be sure and not let go the ropes to get back into the boat; hang by them, no matter where the boat goes, and pull yourself to the step."

Now they were alongside the great black hulk that towered high above them. One of the rowers stood at the bows to prevent the boat being crushed against the ship.

"Are you ready?" asked Will.

"Yes," answered Harry, "when you give the word."

A great wave came sweeping along the ship's side. The boat rose to it and balanced for a moment opposite the steps.

"Now!" shouted Will.

In a moment the wave had passed and the boat was swept down and away; but Harry was swinging in the air, with both hands fast hold of the ropes and both feet on the steps. He clambered up and reached the ship's deck safely. He had little idea what relief Will felt at seeing him there.

As soon as the boat could be brought again into position, Will followed, and the baggage.

As the sun was setting over Syria the "Juno" weighed her anchor, her engines throbbed, under her stern the blades of the propeller churned the water to foam. Slowly gaining headway, the great ship turned her prow to the south and disappeared in the twilight.

CHAPTER XXXII.

EGYPT.

MORNING again at sea! "It seems like old times on the 'Norman Monarch,'" Harry said, "only this is an Austrian ship, instead of a ship under English colors."

Down in the "Juno's" small cabin the air had been close and warm, but up here on deck, with no roof but the sky, the air was to their lungs what the water of bubbling New England springs is for drink. They had been on deck ever since the stars began to fade. There had been a splendid sunrise. They had seen, as Homer would put it, the rosy-fingered dawn leap from her couch beyond the eastern waves. It had the look of a real leap. Will declared he had never seen the like of it except on Eastern waters. It was due, he thought, to the clearness of the air even down close to the horizon. There was no sign of even the least mist.

After a lunch of fresh air they were hungry for something more.

"Let's have them bring us our breakfast here on deck, Cousin Will. I don't believe I could eat a mouthful in the cabin, but now I am as hungry—as those black and white gulls are or pretend to be. Poor fellows! I don't like to cheat them, but watch them now when I throw them a bit of paper."

It was a pretty sight—the graceful sweeping down of the long-winged birds, the excitement, the low calling to each other, and then the trying to seize the white paper as it drifted away in the rough wake of the steamship.

Will ordered their breakfast. It was promptly and nicely served. Jaffa oranges, boiled eggs, delicate Vienna bread, and cups of tea flavored with thin slices of lemon.

An hour later Harry, looking towards the south, suddenly exclaimed,

"Why, Cousin Will, what is that? It looks straight enough and tall enough to be the mast of a ship against the sky, but it is too thick and there is no hull. It might be a rock, but I never saw a rock so like a finger. Can it be a lighthouse?"

Will looked. He was surprised too. "I had not expected it yet," he said, "but it must be the beacon at Port Said, away out at the end of the breakwater that helps form the harbor. Watch, Harry, for soon we will have the first sight of the shore, our first view of Egypt."

FORT SAID.

But when, a little later, they saw the shore, they saw nothing beautiful or imposing. Indeed, in all this part of Egypt there is nothing of natural beauty, and, excepting for man's works, there would be nothing even of special interest. The country is a flat stretch of sand, but through the midst of it man has run the Suez Canal, and here at its terminus he has built Port Said.

Heavy masonry helps to make a good harbor. The town is not at all like most Eastern cities. It is all new, with wide, well-kept streets, wooden houses, broad verandahs, crowds of boats and shipping.

The travellers landed, passed easily with their hand-baggage through the custom house, and found their way to a hotel.

They were accustomed by this time to Oriental ways and Oriental costumes. On a smaller scale there was as much variety of dress here as at the long bridge in Constantinople across the Golden Horn. One novelty, though, was the dress of the negroes—long robes that were white as snow on men tall and stately and black as coals.

There was nothing, except their interest in the canal, to keep the travellers long at Port Said. It did not take much time to inspect the terminal locks and the harbor and the shipping.

Will found that a small steam messenger-boat, which sometimes carried passengers, would start about midnight for Ismailia, half way through the canal. It was just the chance they wanted. It would be dark at starting, but the moon would rise later. The prospect was good for a romantic boat-ride through the desert.

And it was romantic from beginning to end. The romance began when they were called at midnight and found a man waiting outside the hotel to guide them through the almost pitch-dark streets to the boat. Either he was unfamiliar with the way, or the boat was too small for easy finding. At last they discovered the craft. It lay below them, a black little affair, snorting with its small steam-pipes, and with a boisterous crew on board.

"Cousin Will, had n't we better get back to the hotel and wait for daylight?"

"Oh, no, this is just what we want. Halloa down there! Shall we come aboard? Can you hold two men more?"

Some sort of a response came back. They could not tell what, only that it was not English.

"Come on, Harry. Jump carefully for the deck—what there is of one."

So they got aboard. Two or three other passengers and the captain and his crew were in the cabin laughing and talking.

Will and Harry went in and stowed away their baggage. Then they found a good lookout place just in front of the pilot-house. There they settled themselves for the rest of the night. Soon the fastenings were cast off, the men went to their posts, the uproar ceased, and the boat glided out into open water.

The trip was begun. In a few minutes the town was behind them. They were steaming down a long ribbon-like mirror that reflected the stars and nothing else excepting the dim outlines of high banks of sand. Later on a shining face suddenly looked at them over the left bank. It was the moon, come to change the black mirror to silver and to give something more of shape to what were only spectres before — to stakes and passing boats and higher piles of sand.

"Harry, do you know that when they were digging the canal a good part of these miles of sand was carried out just by the basketful on the heads of the natives—the fellaheen?

"But there was room for them all and more in making a canal 100 miles long, 330 feet wide, and 20 feet deep.

"It was a great work, but this is not the first canal that Egypt has had. A long time ago, away back in the time of the Pharaohs, one was begun over this same route. It was a long, long while before it was finished. But that was made not so much for the passage of boats as to be a sort of fortification, a great moat for protection against Asiatic enemies.

"Then there was a very important canal from Alexandria, forty miles across to the Rosetta branch of the Nile. That was rebuilt by Mohammed Ali, and opened in 1820. It was an immense work; 250,000 persons were employed in the digging of it. And so poorly were they cared for that 200,000, it is said, died before it was finished. But it was a great help to Alexandria. It made it practically a port of the Nile."

So, looking and listening and sometimes talking, they watched at the bows of the little boat until the night was gone. When the sun rose, as the moon had risen, everything was changed again. Through breaks in the sand wall they could look off now over the rough surface of the desert. There was no sign of life. But only a little farther on and they came to two great hives of life. They were two huge India steamships that were preparing to get under weigh again after their night's halt. The little despatch-boat, as it ran alongside of them, was like a salmon beside whales.

Half way to Suez, and at the point where the canal widens into Lake Timsah, they reached Ismailia. It is a small station on the railroad from Suez to Cairo and Alexandria.

Here they left the boat, took the first train from Ismailia, whizzed across what was once the Land of Goshen and the home of the Hebrews, and that evening were in Cairo.

CHAPTER XXXIII.

CAIRO.

"Oh, the donkeys, the donkeys, the donkeys. I don't care, Cousin Will, if it is Cairo, and I ought to be thinking about pyramids and greater things. I'm thinking about donkeys, and I can't help it. They are everywhere. Look at that bright little fellow now across the street from us. 'A miserable donkey' indeed! He looks like a little king, with a donkey-boy to wait on him as servant; and he couldn't be better robed—a crimson velvet-lined saddle, silk tassels, silk bridle, well fed, well groomed! If ever again at home I hear donkeys sneered at, I'll just refer the slanderer to the Cairo donkeys for refutation. I don't wonder they are worth as much here as horses, the nicest of them."

"But fine as your donkey is, Harry, suppose you go over and try to hire the little king for work. No doubt that is what it is waiting for. Get two; we shall need them all the time in going about Cairo and out to the Pyramids. To be sure we might take carriages. Would you rather?"

CAIRO, FROM THE CITADEL.

"Indeed I wouldn't. It is bad enough, as it is, to have so much of what might be New York about us—wide streets, modern buildings, nice carriages, European style of dress and stores and hotels. We wont make it seem worse still by ourselves driving about in a carriage, will we? Think of riding that way to the foot of the Pyramids! I expect that some day they will have a railway to the top, and that plenty of folks will prefer that way of mounting them."

"Well, we will not patronize the carriages. Go and get the donkeys. But no, you needn't either. Look there! The boys have seen us, and here they come with a rush, a crowd of them. Whew, what a shouting; swinging arms, dark faces, red caps, white donkeys, black donkeys. Let them keep it up a minute. What a lot of English words and names they have picked up: 'Boston,' 'America,' 'Yankee Doodle,' 'Good donkey,' 'No kick.' There that's enough! We take *you* and *you*. Now the rest of you clear out, and do you two wait here in front of the hotel until we are ready to start."

They sat a while longer on the piazza, watching the panorama of the well-filled street before them.

There was much that was not greatly different from what they had already become familiar with in Oriental towns. Some things were wholly new. It interested them to see the "syces" running before the carriages of dignitaries to clear the way, just as in the old Bible times footmen ran before their masters' chariots. Sometimes two would run side by side, sometimes there would be but one. They were very picturesque, with their bare legs and bright costumes of red and white.

Sometimes an officer of the khedive would ride past, or there would be a line of white uniformed soldiers. Presently they saw approaching from the right a long line of camels. As they reached the space in front of the hotel all at once the man who was leading them seemed greatly troubled, and the camels themselves were frightened.

"What is the matter with them, Cousin Will?"

"I don't know; I see nothing wrong, nothing for them to be afraid of."

"They seem to be afraid to step; they just creep along as though something was hurting them, or as cattle would on ice, or a smooth-shod horse; but we are a long way from ice in this heat. What can it be, I wonder!"

But in a minute Harry had his answer from the camels themselves, poor things! and it was a very plain answer. They had all got safely past excepting the last one in the line. Suddenly that

HASSAN AND DONKEY.

one seemed afraid to even stir; and then when it tried, quick as a flash its legs spread from under it and it sank heavily to the ground, not forward or on its side, but straight down, and in a minute was dead.

"Poor thing! poor thing!" exclaimed Will. "It was the water on the paved street that they were afraid of. I never knew it before, but it seems to be as dangerous to them as ice. And if they do slip, their peculiar build makes them more likely to fall in this ugly position than in a safer way. No wonder it kills them. Their great padded feet were made not for the paved ways, but for the desert and the sand. But we have waited here long enough. Mount your fiery steed, Harry, and we will set out for a donkey ride about the city. Lead the way, Hassan." Hassan was their new guide.

It took but a few minutes to reach a less modern part of the town. Here the streets were narrow and much more Oriental in their aspect; and in the oldest part, in "Old Cairo," there was scarcely anything excepting themselves that was not wholly Egyptian.

They came to a crowd gathered around a juggler and his boy. When the man saw them stop his face brightened with hope of bountiful "backsheesh." He recommenced his programme. He handled poisonous snakes. He seemed to swallow knives and to run a sword down his throat. He forced irons through his flesh. He appeared to draw from his mouth impossibly long coils of cord and ribbons. Then he and the boy twisted themselves into various sorts of knots, with other gymnastic performances. They stayed a while, more to watch the crowd than to see the tricks.

"Before we come to El Azhar, the great school, will you see a little school, sir, a children's school?" asked Hassan.

"If it is near here, yes."

"It is near here, sir."

"Then lead the way."

They came to the place. Leaving the donkeys they climbed a rough flight of stone steps in an old building. The door before them was closed, but as they approached it they heard a great tumult of voices within.

"They must be at recess," remarked Harry, "and having a lively time of it too."

They were admitted. There were some thirty boys sitting there on the floor, and all were busy studying—at the top of their voices. It wasn't recess. If it had been it would have been quieter. To study that way aloud is the custom in all their schools.

They soon returned to the street, and, mounting, jogged on again, with the donkey-boys running behind, up to the citadel and the alabaster mosque of Mohammed Ali. Here there was trouble. The priest in charge of the gateway of the mosque for some reason objected when Hassan proposed to go in.

Hassan was inclined to persist. He only wanted, he said, to cross the court so as to reach a point where they would have a splendid view of the city and the Nile valley.

But "No," the priest said.

"Come on after me," Hassan called to Will and Harry, and was for pushing his way in.

The priest shouted, and half a dozen of his mates came rushing across the court to his help. For a moment, before Will could get to them and interfere, it looked as though there would be a free fight. Hassan was a large, muscular fellow, with an authoritative look and way about him, and apparently very resolute. He was much excited now and seemed to think he could thrash all the priests and force an entrance; and possibly he could have done so had it been worth while.

Will pushed in among them, and, getting in front of Hassan, ordered him back. He reluctantly obeyed, and finally led them by other entrances and passage-ways to the chief points of interest within the large inclosure. But plainly, for some reason, the man they had engaged for their guide was not popular among those who knew him; and this became more and more evident as they went about with him. They found the reason for it later when they were at the Pyramids.

Returning from the citadel and the beautiful mosque, with its walls and columns of pure alabaster, they stopped at what is one of the oldest and largest religious schools in the world. It is the great central school of the Mohammedans for the study of the Koran and all Arabic literature. It is held in the very spacious mosque El Azhar. As one walks among the slender supporting columns, there are seated all about him on the floor hundreds of eager students in small groups around their instructors and leaders. It is said that sometimes there are thousands in attendance at one time, and they come from all parts of the Moslem world.

That afternoon they took a short camel ride outside the city to the "Tombs of the Caliphs." The mosque-like groups of buildings, with their large domes, are imposing from the outside, but within there is very little of interest.

To close the busy day, after tea they found

TOMBS OF THE CALIPHS.

their way through the lighted streets to the pleasant rooms of the American Mission. Dr. Lansing received them very kindly. They were interested in hearing from him of the work of the mission and of its success, especially in the school department. Before leaving they had planned with the doctor the details of a trip to the site of old Memphis and the tombs of the "Sacred Bulls." He would go with them, he said, the first part of the way, on the cars about an hour's ride up the Nile valley to Helwin, where he had work connected with the mission.

When they reached the hotel again and their rooms, they were thoroughly prepared for a night of sound sleep. They were glad too for the quiet and the rest of the Sabbath day that followed.

CHAPTER XXXIV.

A SABBATH DAY IN CAIRO.

The last Sabbath in the East! It dawned as fair as an ideal Sabbath could; and all its hours, from the beginning to its close, seemed to Will and Harry to be ideal also. Yet that was not because the city they were in showed much sign of Sabbath-like rest and peace. Rather it was because there was a real Sabbath day in their hearts. The Sabbath was within them, as the kingdom of God is "within" the Christian. So the day could no more seem altogether like other days, no matter what was about them, than a dark road could seem wholly dark to a man carrying a well-trimmed lamp along it.

Something like that was the thought Will suggested at their morning reading and prayers, before he and Harry came down to breakfast and to the noise and tumult in and about the busy hotel.

Perhaps their philosophy would have been tried, and they too would have become restless, if they had been forced to remain there all day. But to remain indoors was by no means their plan. Not all of Cairo is un-Sunday-like. Very far from it, as they found.

Early in the forenoon they left the hotel. At the foot of the steps the donkey-boys were lying in wait, as usual. They sprang to meet them, as clamorous as ever, but Will waved them away. They would walk this time.

Directly opposite the hotel are the beautiful Ezbekieh Gardens, large, and shaded and adorned with all manner of tropical growth.

There they entered and at once were in comparative quiet. They walked slowly. There was no haste. In some of the pleasantest places among the fountains they sat down and waited, talking quietly. When they left the gardens a few steps more brought them to their destination, the pleasant chapel of the Cairo Mission.

Dr. Lansing had asked Will to meet with the English-speaking congregation in their services for the day, and to talk with them as a Christian visitor from a distant land that they all knew and loved, and that was a fatherland to them in their work for Christ.

Frequent services were to be held during the day. One of them was in progress when Will and Harry entered and quietly took their places in the rear of the large congregation.

They could understand nothing of what was

said. All the exercises were in Arabic, under the lead of the missionaries; but they knew that this company of quiet worshippers were believers in the one God as known through Christ, and that they were only a part of the many who in this land had been helped by the missionaries up to better things. No wonder they honor their teachers and love them; no wonder that these missionaries, like those they had seen in Constantinople and Scutari and Beirût and Sidon, are recognized as a blessing through the entire community where they have made their home!

The Arabic service was followed by another in English. Most of the natives remained, and they were joined by others, residents and visitors in the city. It was pleasant speaking to such an audience. It seemed as though they must be, as they appeared to be, eager to hear and heed. It was like speaking from a far country over great oceans to a little company of those who were brothers because they were Christians. It was like bringing from a land where food is never lacking a few handfuls to those who would have starved but for the earnest working in the vineyard of their small band of God's faithful husbandmen.

At the close of the morning service there was pleasant greeting among those who could no longer seem strangers to each other. The travellers were not allowed to return for the remainder of the Sabbath to the unhomelike hotel. They were welcomed into the missionary circle and home as though they were a part of it.

There were other services before the day closed. It was a full day.

As they walked back through the brief twilight to the hotel, Will said, "Has it been a good day, Harry?"

"Indeed it has, one of our best Sundays."

"And how pleasant it is, Harry, and always will be, for us to think of this and all of the meetings we have had with these Eastern Christians, on Sundays and sometimes on week-days, ever since we left the 'Norman Monarch.' Do you remember the first meeting?"

"Yes, indeed, after we had just landed in Constantinople, when we found the missionaries holding their noon prayer-meeting in the upper story of the Bible House."

"And then that Sunday morning away up on the heights of Scutari, when we met the missionaries in the pleasant parlor of the 'Girls' Home School,' to which so many ladies of New England had given of their wealth and their love; and the prayer-meeting in Beirût; and another Sunday in Damascus, and that evening in Sidon. And then, besides the real Sabbaths, there have been so many times, Harry, that seemed almost as holy and helpful just because of their association. You remember how wonderfully it was so at Mt. Hattîn, where we had our first sudden view of the Sea of Galilee. And that was only one place among the many.

"I tell you, Harry, it ought to help us ahead, it must help us, it must make us better Christians—stronger, gladder, more unselfish, more Christlike every way—to have seen these places, and to have thought of Christ as though he was right with us, as we have done, all the way from the coasts of Tyre and Sidon here to Egypt. These times, scattered along our line of travel, as we look back at them, seem shining way-marks for the road. They are pearl-hours among the common hours. We shall always be the richer for them."

"And this our last Sabbath in Egypt, Cousin Will, is one of the best pearls of them all."

Later in the evening, as they sat in their room, Will had one word more concerning the day and the walk back in the twilight.

"Harry," he said, "it seemed to me, as we were coming home to-night, as though that twilight after such a day was God's benediction to us. It seemed to me something like this;" and he read from a paper he had been pencilling:

TWILIGHT.

The twilight is come;
   The great day-flower
That blossomed at dawn
   From a starry bower
Is fading, faint and slow,
   Unwilling to fold
   Its petals of gold
For the night's benediction low.
The twilight is come.

Now that twilight has come
   And the rose of the day
That blossomed at dawn
   Is fading away,
Hear, Lord, my evening call;
   Thou God of might
   And God of the light,
Let thy peace on my spirit fall,
Now that twilight is come.

He has granted the prayer. He has given
   Me thee, dear Light;
Thyself a most sweet benediction
   From the God of night.

CHAPTER XXXV.

MEMPHIS: TOMBS OF THE SACRED BULLS.

THE travellers are at Helwin. According to plans they had made with Dr. Lansing, they had come up from Cairo the evening before. They had spent the night with him at this little town of the khedive's on the edge of the desert, and now in the very early morning were standing at the door, waiting for the donkey-boys to bring them their steeds.

"Harry," said Cousin Will, "between this sunrise and the next sunset we are likely to have more variety of adventure than on any other day of the few days we spend in Egypt. Here we are on the desert this side of the Nile. We must go down into the 'Valley,' get across the river, pass over the site of old Memphis to the desert again on the other side, the west side. There we shall want to explore the underground 'Tombs of the Sacred Bulls.' Then we will have a long donkey ride down the river, among the fields and villages of the natives, back to Cairo. Here are the donkeys. They wont be as lively when we leave them to-night.

"Good-by, doctor. Thank you again for your care of us."

They set off at a brisk trot, with the boys running behind, ready, according to circumstances, to hasten the donkeys' pace by vigorous pokes with their sticks, or to check it and guide them by pulling at their tails. These boys were small, wiry fellows, who ordinarily could have travelled all day without wearying; but this day gave promise of being terribly hot, and would test the endurance of the whole party.

Indeed, they had not gone far before Will and Harry were glad to add a bit more of color and picturesqueness to the cavalcade by unfurling their bright green and white sun-umbrellas.

"Cousin Will," said Harry, "did you hear the doctor tell me that we could not have travelled here as we are doing now with any sort of comfort, hardly with safety, if it had been as hot as it usually is at this time of the year?"

"Yes. I know the last of May is late for Egypt. We could not stay much longer if we wanted to. But we are fortunate. The weather is cooler, they say, than it has been before in twenty years at this season."

And now they were not far from the Nile.

"Cousin Will, how are we ever to get across the river? I see nothing but a mast ahead. We are not going in a sail-boat, are we? There will be quite a crowd, any way, four of us and two donkeys and all these foot-passengers besides, if they are bound, as they seem to be, the same way with us. I would n't like to be upset and drowned, even if it was in the Nile."

"I knew only that there was some sort of a ferry here, Harry. Apparently that clumsy affair with its big lateen sail is the ferry-boat. There is only a light wind now, but it looks as though a very small puff would be able to capsize the whole affair. There's a crowd on board already, yet they seem to be waiting for us."

They came to the edge of the great river. They had not seen it before, excepting from a distance. It was running swift and muddy along the low, sloping bank.

"It looks like the Mississippi below its junction with the Missouri," said Will.

The boat had grounded five feet or so from the bank.

"How are we to get aboard, Cousin Will? Most everybody is barefoot and can wade conveniently, but I suppose they expect us to walk that narrow plank at the stern. I would rather take a running jump, if only I could be sure of my footing when I struck."

"We had better keep to the plank. But I see

WATER-WHEEL.

no way of getting the donkeys in, unless the boys pick them up and hand them in as they would a sheep, or else follow the tactics which those donkey-boys of Gibraltar adopted."

The latter method was the one they followed. The donkeys would not step into the water, but facing them towards the boat, the boys pushed from behind until they had to jump. They came aboard safely. The drivers clambered after, and all was ready for the crossing to the opposite bank.

With much shouting, and with much creaking and swaying of boom and mast, that voyage was safely accomplished. It was easy disembarking, but then there was a hard scramble up the bank, which on this side is very steep and high.

Safely up, they came at once into the midst of rich fields of grain and groves of great palms, date-palms, but not now in fruit. Close by a "shadoof" was at work, slowly raising the water for irrigating the land. A short distance away, under the trees, was a small village of square huts called "Mitrahenny."

As they rode on they knew, although for a long time there was no slightest evidence of it about them, that they were riding over the site of what was once the very chief of the cities of

Egypt, ancient Memphis, the Noph and Moph of Scripture.*

Said Will, "How strange to think that where we are riding now once great Memphis rose, the capital of Egypt for nearly a thousand years under the shepherd kings, as well as later under other dynasties. Its circuit was seventeen miles. Immense temples were in it—to Isis, to Serapis, to the Sun. It was the centre of Egypt for politics, for learning, for religion. Yet see what it is now—a sort of fertile farm, this part of it, and farther on a desert. The city had so entirely disappeared that for a long, long time no one ever even suspected that this was its site; and when at last a few began to make the claim it was hard to feel certain about it. Some accepted the theory, and some said it could not be a true one."

"I don't wonder. Are they certain now? I don't see how they can be."

"Yes, they are certain. The proof, when it came, was very plain and very interesting. You know that one of the chief of the gods of the Egyptians was the sacred bull Apis.† Now an ancient historian, Strabo, in describing Memphis,

---

* Isa. 19:13; Jer. 2:16; 46:14, 19; Ezek. 30:13, 16; Hosea 9:6.

† These bulls were black, with certain white spots on the face and side.

MEMPHIS: TOMBS OF SACRED BULLS. 313

had said that the approach to the temple, and to the great underground tomb of the Bulls, was through a splendid colonnade of Sphinxes. But what had become of this colonnade? There seemed to be no signs of it here. No wonder that men said this could not be the place.

"But one day, as lately as 1860, an antiquarian and explorer named M. Mariette came across what appeared to him to be the head of a Sphinx just showing above the drifting sand.

"M. Mariette remembered the old description of Strabo. He was greatly excited, as he might well be. If he could find that avenue, and the temple and the tomb, where for 1,500 years the bulls had been worshipped when alive and solemnly buried when dead, it would be a notable discovery. It would make the identification of the site complete and would reveal many other things of value and interest. If he could find what he hoped for! But could he?

"He began digging eagerly, deeper and deeper. He was n't after gold, but after what seemed to him much better than gold. And what do you suppose he found?

"As he dug through the sand, sometimes seventy feet below the surface, lo, one after another the sphinxes appeared, until one hundred and forty-one were uncovered, and the pedestals of many more that had been overthrown. And besides, although the temple to which they once led could not be found, he did find the great Tomb of the Bulls. We shall come to it presently. That is our goal, as it was his."

"Get up, donkeys! Punch them, boys! Hurry on to the Tombs!" shouted Harry.

And so away they went on the run over the rich black soil of the Nile plain, but it was only for a short time.

"Whoa! whoa! Look out there, Cousin Will! But was n't I near riding head and heels, donkey and all, into that hole! What can anybody want here of a hole of that bigness? It might be the grave of a fifty-foot giant. O Cousin Will, look there! It's enough to frighten one. Look down there! There is the giant himself!"

"There he is, sure enough. Well, this is a discovery, Harry. I was n't expecting it, though I know now what it is. Here's a break in the ground where we can get down to the old statue, for it is old, as old as the time of Moses. There, now we are down and can examine it in detail. Do you see how fine the face is, and how carefully the whole was carved and polished? It is badly battered now, but it was a splendid statue when it stood, fifty feet high, in front of the temple of Phtah. It lies in the mud now, and you and your donkey were near tumbling over it—this once proud statue of Rameses the Great, who reigned 4,000 years ago and conquered nations and built temples and cities. Truly, Harry, a very appropriate scripture to think of here is that word of Isaiah: 'Is this the man that made the earth to tremble, that did shake kingdoms; that made the world as a wilderness, and destroyed the cities thereof, that opened not the house of his prisoners? All the kings of the nations, even all of them, lie in glory, every one in his own house. But thou art cast out of thy grave like an abominable branch, and as the raiment of those that are slain, thrust through with a sword, that go down to the stones of the pit.'" Isa. 14 : 16–19.*

They clambered out of the pit and in somewhat quieted mood proceeded on their way.

Soon they reached the desert again. They had crossed the fertile valley. That was all behind them. Their path now led in and out among high mounds of drifted sand that often were full of broken pieces of brick and bits of crockery from the ruins of the vanished city. It was slow travelling, and hard and hot.

In the midst of these sand-drifts, where there

---

* According to many writers it was the daughter of this Rameses II., called the Great, who took Moses from the bulrushes.

was no sign of verdure or of ordinary habitation, suddenly they came upon a square-built house with wide veranda and low roof, shaded and quiet and cool, and with Arabs coming and going about it.

This was the well-kept station of those who, for the present, had the care and charge of the "Tombs of the Sacred Bulls."

Will and Harry were glad to dismount and rest. The shade and the drinks of cool water that were brought were needed refreshment.

When at length they were ready to explore the tombs, one of the Arabs, after taking from its place a heavy key and a candle, signed to them to follow him.

He led the way until they came to a steep descent dug through the yielding sand and walled on either side. At the bottom a massive door was unlocked and opened. The candle was lighted, they descended a flight of steps, and were in the tomb, deep under ground, in what would have been absolute darkness but for the little glimmer of light in the hand of the Arab. The air was close.

"Cousin Will," whispered Harry, "I believe this is going to be worse than the time we had in those caves under Jerusalem."

However, they soon forgot the strangeness in

the interest of what they saw. The place they found to be a long tunnel hewn through solid rock for more than a third of a mile, but with the accessible part something over two hundred yards in length. On each side of the tunnel are chambers, and for each chamber there is a huge granite sarcophagus. Most of these sarcophagi remain where they were placed when the carefully-embalmed bulls were placed within them. They are made from single blocks of stone, very highly polished, and covered all over with delicate hieroglyphics telling of the birth and history and death and burial of the dead god—the bull mummy which they once contained. They were all closed originally with heavy granite covers.

An effort was made a few years ago to remove one of these sarcophagi to the Egyptian museum at Boulak, but the undertaking failed. They succeeded in moving it into the main passage; there they left it. Its great weight made it impossible for them to drag it up the inclined plane to the surface. Yet these same blocks had been brought to Memphis by the workmen of those times, nearly six hundred miles from the quarries of Syene.

"Cousin Will, do n't you suppose it was partly because the children of Israel had seen the Egyptians worshipping these bulls that they were so ready to make that golden calf at Mt. Sinai and to worship it?"

"Yes. It was natural that if they began to long for a visible object of worship, what they had seen of the Egyptians' reverence for the sacred bull helped to incline them towards making a similar image to represent the unseen Jehovah. But, Harry, you must not think that the bull was the only animal reverenced by the Egyptians. Many others were worshipped, though not as widely nor with as much of splendor. For instance, there was a species of ibis that was worshipped almost everywhere. Its carefully-preserved mummies are found by the million, though the bird itself has now become extinct. Crocodiles, monkeys, snakes—all had their devotees."

"Cousin Will, here's a step-ladder. Can't I get up and climb over into one of the sarcophagi?"

"Yes, if you want to, into this one; its cover is partly off. There is no mummy in there now."

Harry climbed in. There was plenty of room. The space was large and the sides were smoothly and evenly cut. Soon he scrambled out.

They had seen enough, and retraced their steps. They were glad to regain the light and air of the upper world.

While they rested again at the station they

talked of many things—of what they had just seen, with all that it suggested, and of the neighboring "Pyramids of Sakkari." There are eleven of these pyramids in the midst of what was once an immense graveyard of the Egyptians. One of the eleven, the "Stepped Pyramid," some think is even older than the Great Pyramids of Ghizeh. Its shape is unique, for the base, instead of being square, is oblong, and it has the peculiar "stepped sides."

But as Harry and Will talked it seemed to them that there was one series of events in the long and strange history of the region about them that was grander in itself and in its results than anything besides that had ever occurred there.

"Just think, Harry. Imagine again what all this region once was, how it was teeming with life and splendor, a great royal city, and then remember that it was here probably that Moses and Aaron came to tell Pharaoh that he must let their people go; here that the plagues fell; here that the first-born died; here that the mighty king yielded at last before a mightier Jehovah, and with all his people hastened to obey and to let God's people depart from this land of their terrible bondage. 'Pharaoh rose up in the night, he and all his servants, and all the Egyptians. . . . . And he called for Moses and Aaron by night, and said, Rise up and get you forth from among my people, both ye and the children of Israel; and go, serve the Lord as ye have said. ... And the Egyptians were urgent upon the people, that they might send them out of the land in haste.' Ex. 12 : 30–33.

"But we have rested long enough; it is time for us to go, Harry."

They bade the Arabs good-by, remounted their donkeys, and set out on their long ride down the valley to Cairo.

All the afternoon they rode. The drivers lost their way among the many intersecting paths and canals and embankments; but there was no loss in that excepting of time. It gave a better opportunity for seeing the country, and the people at work and in their homes. They knew the general direction they were to take.

They found no waste land. Every spot was cultivated. In places the people were threshing their grain in primitive fashion, just as in Bible times, by driving oxen with drags over and over the threshing-floor. Others were harrowing throwing the grain high in the air, that so the wind might separate it from the chaff. Here and there a camel passed loaded with straw, and donkeys carrying produce to Cairo.

The afternoon lengthened. It was very hot.

They rode slowly, for their own comfort and out of pity for the tired donkey-boys and their tired beasts. In one place—it was near the fine bridge by which they recrossed the Nile—Will's donkey stumbled and partly fell. If it had been a horse there might have been a serious accident. As it was, Will's feet were so near the ground he simply found himself standing over the fallen steed, with nothing to do but to step over his head and wait until he righted himself.

It was long after dark when they dismounted in front of their hotel. The day had been a full day, but a satisfactory one.

"Here, boys, is your pay," said Will, handing them a liberal backsheesh.

They took the money, glanced at it, and thrust it back into his hand with gestures and words of intense disgust.

Will laughed; he received the money quietly instead of arguing with them as they had expected, and slipping it into his pocket, turned away and mounted the steps of the hotel with Harry.

He was hardly across the piazza and at the door before the boys were at his side with all imaginable meekness and humility, begging him to give them whatever he chose.

He paid them and they were gone.

CHAPTER XXXVI.

THE PYRAMIDS.

"Harry, if all goes well, this will be one of the white days of our trip. Think of at last climbing the Pyramids! A year ago, at home, you had no reason for supposing you would ever see them. They seemed farther away than the moon—which at any rate was in sight; yet here we are ready to mount the two donkeys which have the glory, that they do not appreciate, of being the last of the long succession of our carriers between New Haven and the base of Cheops. The 'Norman Monarch' was the first. These two Cairo donkeys are the last. All honor to them. I hope they will bear us well.

"Come on. There is Hassan striding down the pathway, majestic in black tasseled fez and loose robe of silk, baggy trousers, white stockings, and yellow slippers. He turns out of the way for nobody. He might be owner of a good part of Cairo or the whole of it, or partner of the khedive. See him cuff the donkey-boys. They seem quite in awe of him.

"Good morning, Hassan; why are you so free with your fists?"

"It's the best way, sir. It's the only way to get along with the natives, sir."

"Do you think so? But while you are with us don't be quite so ready to use that method as you were the other day at the Alabaster Mosque."

"I wont, sir."

Soon they were mounted and off for the Pyramids. Out of the city, across the Nile bridge, westward they went.

As they rode Harry asked, "Cousin Will, you called one of the Pyramids the Pyramid of Cheops. Why has it that name?"

"Of the seventy Pyramids in Egypt, the three at Ghizeh, where we are bound now, are the finest; and of the three, the Pyramid of Cheops is the most interesting. It takes its name from the monarch who built it. It is the largest of them all. It covers thirteen acres. It is supposed that 100,000 men were at work on it for thirty years. Cheops built it for his sepulchre, 2,000 years or more before the time of Christ."

They were hardly more than clear of the city before they saw away in front of them, still and massive and clear cut against the sky, the familiar picture, the original of what they had so often seen in books and on canvas. There before them were those works of man which for massiveness are the nearest like works of God of anything that men have ever made.

Were they disappointed in this distant view of them? Indeed they were!

"O Cousin Will," exclaimed Harry, "I do n't know but I would rather never have seen them at all than to have seen them so much less than I anticipated! 'Mountains of rock' indeed! 'wonders of the ages!' I feel as though it was a fraud; as though somebody had been cheating me. Hardly that though. It is more that I feel just sorry and disappointed. Do n't you feel so, Cousin Will?"

"Yes, I do. And yet when we come to think about it, they must be farther away than they seem to us to be in this clear atmosphere; and if that is so, we can easily understand why they appear now to be so small. Do you know the philosophy of it? Whenever one sees an object and is about to judge of its size, there is always first an involuntary estimate concerning its distance. A baby, because he thinks that the moon is within reach, thinks also that it is small enough to be grasped by his chubby little hands. Have you not sometimes looked up suddenly through a closed window and thought you saw a large bird far away among the clouds or over the tree-tops, but instead it was only a tiny fly crawling along the pane? So in looking at the Pyramids, the rays of light that come from them enter into our eyes at a certain angle and form the picture on the retina. We have to judge of the distance. If we imagine that they are very much nearer to us than they really are, we cannot help at the same time judging them to be very much smaller than they really are. If we could realize that they are many miles away, and yet are large enough to fill this angle of vision, we would easily appreciate them as immense."

Two hours' ride from Cairo, with frequent interruptions from unrepaired paths, brought the travellers to the foot of the great hills of stone.

A crowd of Arabs flocked around them as they approached, some of them eager to take charge of the donkeys, others as eager to be hired as guides and assistants to the top, others trying to sell little mementos—seals and charms and idols—which they declared they had found in the tombs, but which more likely were all of English make.

The Arabs were quieted somewhat and induced to give space with the help of Hassan. Hassan they seemed to know well and to look at askance. Plainly, besides having no liking for him, they were rather afraid of him.

The travellers rested a while on their blankets

spread over the sand before undertaking the ascent.

"What do you say now, Harry, to the height of the Pyramids?" asked Will, as they lay looking up the more than four hundred and fifty feet of rock stairs that sloped above them.

"I say this is very much more like what I expected, yet it is n't quite all that I hoped for. However, I do n't complain. I am satisfied; and I imagine that before we get to the top I will be more than satisfied. It will be like climbing a small mountain. Whew! would n't it have been a great place once for sliding down hill when it was covered smoothly from top to bottom with polished stone! I believe I shall be half afraid now of falling, and having not a slide, but a very bumping roll, before we are through. How uneven the steps are, Cousin Will! from two feet to four or five, are n't they? And the color of the rock! I thought it was dark, and instead it is almost white—a sort of cream color."

"Yes, it is all made of a light limestone, excepting in places along the passages and in the lining of the inner chambers; there a very hard granite-like rock is used. Well, are you rested? If you are, now for the climb. How much help do you want, Harry?"

"The Arabs seem to think I want them

all. Do you suppose I really need any of them?"

"Indeed you do. We will have two of them apiece. They will help by climbing ahead and then pulling us up step by step. We will dispense with the third fellow who wants to go behind and push.

"Now you four men—*you* and *you* and *you* and *you*, understand—just you four and no others, are the men we hire; and understand again, only when we are through with you will we pay you. The rest of you can go along if you want the climb, but not one backsheesh will the rest of you get from us."

Nevertheless a good part of the whole tribe did go with them to the very top. It was in the vain hope that their frequent offers of help and of water and of food would at last be appreciated and accepted. Hassan was to stay behind.

"Now, Harry, here at this corner is the starting-place. Up we go. Don't hurry, and be sure and stop—don't forget this—be sure and stop, no matter how often, whenever you are in the least out of breath or tired."

It was exciting work—the light-robed Arabs, dark, agile, quick as cats, springing along the easiest places, then reaching down with their bare muscular arms to Will and Harry; a strong clasp of hands; a half step and a half spring; higher and higher! Once as they held him Harry missed his footing. There was hardly a hand's breadth any way to rest upon. As he stepped he lost his balance and swung sharply to the right. It would have been a bad fall, but quick as a flash the Arabs braced back against the wall. They kept their grip on his hands. Another pull, and he was safely up on the broader step at their side.

Half way to the summit they stopped for a long rest. It seemed to them that from this point the pyramid was more awe-inspiring than from any other place. Now there was a great slope below them as well as above them. They were like a little group of ants clinging to a huge wall. Here at last, where they had least expected it, they found that the sense of immensity and grandeur and majesty was all and more than they had ever anticipated.

Presently they were climbing again, and soon they were at the summit. The apex of the pyramid has been broken away. The top now is a roughly-levelled platform a few feet square. Looking down and off from this height the travellers could see their donkeys at the foot of the pyramid like mice and the men like pigmies; they could mark the clear-cut line where the sand curved in and out against the green of the fertile Nile valley. On the one side of them the bare desert stretched away as far as they could see, shining yellow in the sunlight; on the other side were the Nile and Cairo and scattered villages and fertile fields. Close beside them, and rather above their level because of its higher foundation and its unbroken apex, towered the second pyramid. A part of its smooth casing is still in place near the summit. One of the persistent Arabs, noticing that they were talking about this pyramid, eagerly offered his services. He was earnest to be allowed to entertain them by running down one pyramid and up the other.

"It will be great fun," he declared; "I will do it in a minute. I will do it for one franc—I will do it for half a franc."

"Harry, we must get rid of them in some way. They are too troublesomely talkative. As though we cared for their monkey antics on the pyramids and their gossip and jokes in broken English!

"Away with you, all of you! Go down; go down five steps; so many—as many as my fingers—and stay there until I say, Come. Go!"

Then they had peace. They talked but little to each other; but when it was time to descend Will said,

"Harry, we ought to be better men for what

these pyramids and the desert and the great Nile valley have been saying to us, better men for what God has been saying to us through them. I have been thinking how—great and old as it all is—it is not as lasting and as grand as are the souls of the millions who have lived and died here, not as lasting and as wonderful as our own souls, Harry. The men that built these huge monuments built up at the same time their own character and destiny, and these will last on when the pyramids themselves are no more."

"How wonderful! And isn't it just so with us too, Cousin Will?"

"Yes, indeed. And how careful we ought to be to build aright!"

The descent was easy, comparatively, and rapid. They reached the base without mishap.

In the distance Hassan was seen approaching. The Arabs, who had flocked around again with their calls for backsheesh and offers of relics, suddenly quieted at sight of him, and as he strode nearer drew off with dark looks. But as they went one of them muttered to Will,

"That man bad. We no like him. He no good Mohammedan. He bad man. He drink whiskey. He fight."

"Ah, Harry, that tells the story. To their credit be it said, no true Mussulman will drink alcoholic liquors. Plainly Hassan uses them. They know it, and hate him as a renegade. Moreover, he fights; so, besides hating him, they are afraid of him. I doubt, though, if it is fear alone that makes them shun him. They are sensible; they do not want to get into a needless quarrel.

"It is noon; we have had exercise enough to make us hungry. Hassan, find a good place and spread the lunch."

They rested an hour or so. Then Will said,

"Now it is time to explore the interior of the pyramid. We will find the 'King's Chamber.'"

They climbed to the entrance in the side of the pyramid, a dark hole opening into the stone. Once probably there was an imposing entranceway. A narrow passage leads beyond. They crept along carefully, with an Arab in front carrying a dim candle, and a line of Arabs behind. Much of the way they had to stoop as they went under the low ceiling. In one place a shaft, black and deep, opened directly in their path. They could advance only by climbing past it along a narrow shelf at the side.

"Evidently," remarked Harry, "whoever built this did not mean it to be a thoroughfare."

"Indeed they did not," said Will. "They

worked hard to hide their inner chambers and to secure them for ever from all possible intrusion. If the Pyramids are sepulchres, their builders meant that no intruder should ever find and disturb their embalmed bodies after they were once entombed."

At the very centre of the pyramid the tunnel which they had been following opened suddenly into what in the dimness seemed to be a very lofty and spacious chamber.

"For one franc I illuminate," exclaimed an Arab.

"Illuminate, then," answered Will.

The fellow had picked up somewhere a bit of magnesium. As he touched it with a match and the light from it flashed out clear and strong, the walls and ceiling of the chamber seemed to approach, as though to shut them in and make an undesired sarcophagus for them all. Really the place is a room some 34 feet long by 17 wide and 19 high, lined smoothly throughout with great blocks of granite-like stone.

The light gleamed brightly for only a few seconds; then the sarcophagus seemed darker than ever. That Arab was a fraud, but the bargain had been made and he received his promised reward.

Near the centre of the chamber, and the only

thing in it, is a large block of stone, hollowed and fitted to receive a cover. There have been various theories as to what it is. Probably it is a sarcophagus and once contained the body of the royal builder of the pyramid.

There was nothing to keep them long in this uncanny place. The candle was burning low; the air was heavy with the fumes from the "illumination." They were ready to get outside as soon as possible.

Suddenly there was a little puff. The candle was out. They were in absolute darkness. They could not see an inch before them. Harry had been roaming about the chamber, but just then, fortunately, he was standing near Will. Will clutched him; then they waited.

The silence was as absolute as the darkness.

But in a minute a voice spoke.

"We can't get out. You pay us large backsheesh and we try."

Will's answer was entirely effective. First they heard the sharp double click of his revolver. They easily understood what that meant. Then he said,

"Now, fellows, we don't want any of this. I understand just what you are after, but it is of no use. You think you can frighten us into giving you money, as you frightened the Englishman you had in here the other day. But, as it happens, you are the ones that have most reason to be afraid. Such tricks are not safe play now-a-days. Now light that candle, and be quick about it; it's getting late."

And they were quick. They protested it was all a joke, just for fun; they would do so no more. And during the remainder of the day they were model attendants. They retraced their steps without further adventure.

Later they went with Hassan and the still persevering retinue of Arabs off 300 feet east of the second pyramid to where the Sphinx crouches in its bed of drifting sand, or, rather, on its rock-bed, with robes of drifted sand about it.

"What a strange, strange creature it is," said Harry, when they had walked around it and were standing at last facing it where the sand slopes up from its front. "It makes me feel as solemn as an ancient sage to look at it, it is so old and still and strange—part bird and part man and part beast."

"It would seem stranger still, Harry, if we could see the whole of it. Now, with the sand drifted half way over its body, there is nothing to show that underneath is a large platform of the native rock, and that between its fore paws is a little temple for the use of worshippers. This

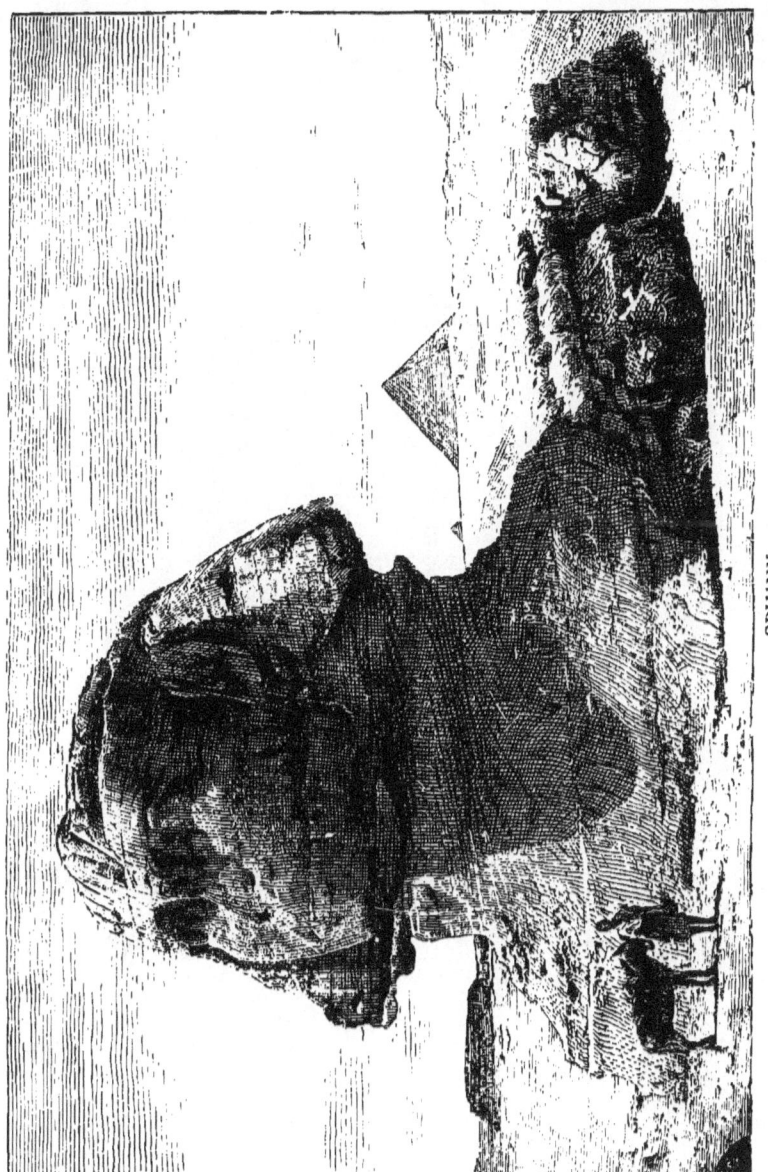

SPHINX.

fine sand is as hard to deal with as snow; harder, for this lasts where snow would melt.

"Who carved and built the Sphinx no one knows. You see it is made partly from the solid rock and partly from masonry, in all about 172 feet long and 56 feet high. It must be at least as old as the Pyramids. Neither do we know the meaning of it, unless it is a sort of symbol of the power and wisdom perhaps of Egypt, perhaps of their kings, perhaps of their gods."

They lingered long about these mighty relics. The shadows from them were stretching far away towards the Nile when at last they called Hassan to bring the donkeys. They mounted and rode away—away from the Pyramids, away from the great, silent Sphinx, away from the clamor of the Arabs. They turned often for a last look, but in good time were safely back in the busy city. It was their last day in the neighborhood of Cairo.

CHAPTER XXXVII.

ALEXANDRIA.—HOME.

ANOTHER fair morning, but most of it was to be spent on the cars. There was an early good-by to the pleasant friends they had made in Cairo. They drove to the station. The train was ready. In a few moments Cairo and the Pyramids and the Sphinx all were behind them. They were speeding away swiftly northward towards Alexandria. Another day and Alexandria also would be behind them and they afloat again on the blue Mediterranean.

They left Cairo at 8 A. M. Early in the afternoon they were skirting the great, shallow Lake Mareotis. At 2 o'clock they were in Alexandria. After a good dinner at the Hotel de l' Europe, facing the pleasant Frank Square, they went to the office of the Italian Steamship Company and bought their tickets for the steamer that was to sail the next day.

As they left the office a crowd of boys with their donkeys began clamoring at the edge of the sidewalk. They chose the two best-looking beasts, mounted, and jogged away along the wide and modern-looking streets.

"Where shall we go, Cousin Will?"

"Anywhere that the donkeys and their drivers want to take us. We must see "Pompey's Pillar." Besides that there is very little now of much interest in Alexandria. Cleopatra's Needles, that used to stand down by the water, and that are 3,000 years old, are both gone—one to England and the bank of the Thames, the other to America, to Central Park in New York. We might visit the excavations under the city, but after what we have seen elsewhere they would not be of much interest; besides it would take more time than we have to spare."

"Start your donkeys towards Pompey's Pillar, boys."

"It seems strange, Harry, how little there is left of this that was once one of the greatest cities of the world. When Alexander the Great conquered Egypt, 300 years before Christ, he changed the capital from Memphis to this place. Before there had been nothing here excepting a poor little village. But at once the village sprang into a great and splendid city. Soon it had some 600,000 inhabitants. There were palaces and temples and museums and libraries. Its library came to be the very largest of ancient times. There were in it 400,000 volumes or rolls, some say 700,000. Think of that many, all made by hand! Part of them were burned when Julius Cæsar besieged the city. Others were preserved for a while in the great heathen temple of Jupiter Serapis; but when that last of the heathen temples was destroyed, in the time of Theodosius the Great, most of the manuscripts went with it; and the last were lost when the Arabs came and captured the city in the seventh century. There have been vast changes in the fortunes of the place. There has been much fighting over it. It has had many masters.

"One great result of Alexander's choice of a seaport for the capital was the changing the nation almost at once into a great maritime and commercial power. Previously they had been almost entirely an agricultural people. Very soon the harbor was one of the busiest places in the Mediterranean. It was crowded with shipping. A good part of the trade of the world passed there. At its entrance, on the island of Pharos, they built their famous lighthouse—the most famous of ancient times. There is no island there now. The space has all filled in between it and the shore, so that what was an island is now a part of the mainland. But on the point there will shine to-night, just as there shone 2,000 years ago, a brilliant and much-needed light."

At last they approached Pompey's Pillar.

It stands alone, a tall sentinel on a slight rise of ground somewhat out from the newer part of the city. It is made of reddish granite. The length of the shaft is 73 feet. The whole height is a little short of 100 feet.

"Why is it called Pompey's Pillar, Cousin Will?"

"That title is a misnomer. An inscription in Greek tells that it was the work of an Egyptian governor, Publius by name, and that he erected it not in the honor of Pompey, but of the Emperor Diocletian. That was about 500 years ago. So, compared with some of the monuments we have seen, Pompey's Pillar is no more than a baby in age."

Not far from the pillar is an entrance to some of the excavations beneath the city. Just as Will and Harry were riding away a guide appeared. He was very earnest in trying to persuade them to explore these subterranean passages under his lead. According to him, they would miss a great deal if they refused. But, apparently much to his surprise, they resisted the temptation. Turning away, they rode back to the city and to their hotel.

They sat late that night enjoying the fragrant air and the night sounds—some of them. The occasional howling of the near dogs was not enjoyable, but the noisiest ones were far away, far enough away for distance to lend something of enchantment even to them. The street calls and cries, a sound from somewhere of musical instruments and voices, the twitter now and then of a bird, and the hum of insects—it was all very peaceful and restful. It was a pleasant evening for the last evening in Egypt. And the last "good night" before they were asleep was the muezzin call from a slim minaret against the sky:

"God is most great! There is no deity but God! Mohammed is the apostle of God! Come to prayer! Come to security! God is most great! There is no deity but God."

It seemed to Harry that he had been asleep about two minutes when he opened his eyes and found the room full of morning sunlight. Will was up moving quietly about, packing their hand boxes and strapping the shawls and wraps.

"Awake, are you, Harry? Was it I or the sun that did it? No matter. I would have called you in a minute any way."

"Is it a good day for sailing, Cousin Will? Is it still? I hope we'll not have as rough water as we had at Jaffa."

"There is hardly a breath of wind. Instead of being tossed towards the sky, up and down among great waves, we are likely to go rowing out to

ALEXANDRIA.

our steamship over water that is like a mirror. We wont have to practise gymnastics and risk a wetting in getting on board the 'India,' as we had in boarding the 'Juno.' "

After breakfast they drove to the custom house. A block away they were besieged by porters, clamoring to be allowed to carry their small amount of luggage. One of them sprang up and clung to the side of the carriage as they drove.

They reached the custom house doors, rescued their boxes from the many hands that were grasping at them, entered, and handed over the luggage for the inspection of the officials. There was a slight examination, a few questions were asked, nothing contraband was found. They paid the required fee and passed on towards the crowd of boats waiting for passengers at the stone steps. Here the hubbub recommenced, or, rather, swelled again, for it had not wholly ceased since they came in sight. There was not much choice in the boats. All were in good order. They selected one.

"How much to the 'India'?"

"That all right, sir. Get in, get in."

"No; tell me how much."

"Anything; what you choose, sir; we fix that afterwards."

"Do as I say, or hand out the luggage. We can take another boat."

At once a dozen more boats were offered. But now the first boatmen were entirely submissive.

"Get in; all right. Five franc each."

"One franc and no more."

"Yes, yes; one franc; all right."

There was no more delay or trouble. The amount named was the regular fee for such service. The men could have no excuse now for stopping, as they sometimes do, midway between the shore and the ship to haggle about the price and demand payment. They pulled steadily and rapidly out from among the smaller craft, over the still water, past larger ships at anchor. Here there was more room, and the four muscular fellows made the oars bend and the water foam as they drove their boat ahead. They were early. If they hastened they might be back in time for another trip with more passengers.

They reached the ship. In the sheltered harbor, and with a breeze so light that it only made "cats' paws" here and there over the surface, the great "India" lay as motionless as though she was an island shaped like a ship. They easily climbed the steps to her deck. The oarsmen were paid. They scrambled back to their tiny-looking little boat, pushed off, and sped away rapidly towards the distant pier.

Will and Harry went below to their state-room to make all ready for the voyage. Soon they returned to the quarter-deck. Resting there under an awning that sheltered them from the sun, which would be burning hot at mid-day, they waited, watching the changing picture about them. Other boats were coming and going, some with passengers and some with freight. There was more and more of interest and of action as the time approached for sailing.

By noon the time had come. All was ready. The signal was given to clear the ship. The small boats rowed quickly away, and, as they rowed, the very last good-by from Egypt sounded in the shoutings of their tawny crew.

Another signal from the captain. A bell tinkled in the engine-room below; and in a moment what had just been like an island in the form of a ship was alive in every part. The "India" turned slowly, gathered headway, and soon was surging swiftly northward, past the tower of the "Pharos Light," out into the calms and the storms of the Mediterranean.

Will and Harry were to travel for a few months more in other lands, but their pleasant journeying together in the Orient was ended.

On one of the last days of August the steamship "Bolivia," from Edinburgh, slowed down to receive her pilot in a thick fog off New York harbor. The next morning she steamed inside of Sandy Hook, past the Highland lights, up the lower bay, and through the Narrows towards her berth at the foot of Dey Street, New York city. Standing by the railing on her upper deck were Harry and Will. A few hours later and they were in the midst of a welcome such as only home can give.

www.ingramcontent.com/pod-product-compliance
Lightning Source LLC
Chambersburg PA
CBHW030345230426
43664CB00007BB/535